First Print Edition [1.0] -1440h. (2018c.e.)

Copyright © 1440 H./2018 C.E.
Taalib al-Ilm Educational Resources

http://taalib.com
Learn Islaam, Live Islaam.^{SM}

All rights reserved, this publication may be not reproduced, stored in a retrieval system, or transmitted in any form or by any means, electronic, mechanical, photocopying, recording, scanning, or otherwise, except with the prior written permission of the Publisher.

Requests to the Publisher for permission should be addressed to the Permissions Department, Taalib al-Ilm Educational Resources by e-mail: **service@taalib.com**.

Taalib al-Ilm Education Resources products are made available through distributors worldwide. To view a list of current distributors in your region, or information about our distributor/referral program please visit our website. Discounts on bulk quantities of our products are available to community groups, religious institutions, and other not-for-profit entities, inshAllaah. For details and discount information, contact the special sales department by e-mail: **service@taalib.com**.

The publisher requests that any corrections regarding translations or knowledge based issues, be sent to us at: **service@taalib.com**. Readers should note that internet websites offered as citations and/or sources for further information may have changed or no longer be available between the time this was written and when it is read. We publish a variety of full text and free preview edition electronic ebook formats. Some content that appears in print may not be available in electronic book versions.

ISBN EAN-13:   978-1-938117-79-4   [Soft cover Print Edition]

From the Publisher

GOLDEN WORDS UPON GOLDEN WORDS...FOR EVERY MUSLIM.

"Imaam al-Barbahaaree, may Allaah have mercy upon him said:

May Allaah have mercy upon you! Examine carefully the speech of everyone you hear from in your time particularly. So do not act in haste and do not enter into anything from it until you ask and see: Did any of the Companions of the Prophet, may Allaah's praise and salutations be upon him, speak about it, or did any of the scholars? So if you find a narration from them about it, cling to it, do not go beyond it for anything and do not give precedence to anything over it and thus fall into the Fire.

Explanation by Sheikh Saaleh al-Fauzaan, may Allaah preserve him:

'Do not be hasty in accepting as correct what you may hear from the people especially in these later times. As now there are many who speak about so many various matters, issuing rulings and ascribing to themselves both knowledge and the right to speak. This is especially the case after the emergence and spread of new modern day media technologies.

Such that everyone now can speak and bring forth that which is in truth worthless; by this meaning words of no true value - speaking about whatever they wish in the name of knowledge and in the name of the religion of Islaam. It has even reached the point that you find the people of misguidance and the members of the various groups of misguidance and deviance from the religion speaking as well. Such individuals have now become those who speak in the name of the religion of Islaam through means such as the various satellite television channels. Therefore be very cautious!

It is upon you oh Muslim, and upon you oh student of knowledge individually, to verify matters and not rush to embrace everything and anything you may hear. It is upon you to verify the truth of what you hear, asking, 'Who else also makes this same statement or claim?', 'Where did this thought or concept originate or come from?', 'Who is its reference or source authority?'. Asking what are the evidences which support it from within the Book and the Sunnah? And inquiring where has the individual who is putting this forth studied and taken his knowledge from? From who has he studied the knowledge of Islaam?

Each of these matters requires verification through inquiry and investigation, especially in the present age and time. As it is not every speaker who should rightly be considered a source of knowledge, even if he is well spoken and eloquent, and can manipulate words captivating his listeners. Do not be taken in and accept him until you are aware of the degree and scope of what he possesses of knowledge and understanding. As perhaps someone's words may be few, but possess true understanding, and perhaps another will have a great deal of speech yet he is actually ignorant to such a degree that he doesn't actually posses anything of true understanding. Rather he only has the ability to enchant with his speech so that the people are deceived. Yet he puts forth the perception that he is a scholar, that he is someone of true understanding and comprehension, that he is a capable thinker, and so forth. Through such means and ways he is able to deceive and beguile the people, taking them away from the way of truth.

Therefore what is to be given true consideration is not the amount of the speech put forth or that one can extensively discuss a subject. Rather the criterion that is to be given consideration is what that speech contains within it of sound authentic knowledge, what it contains of the established and transmitted principles of Islaam. As perhaps a short or brief statement which is connected to or has a foundation in the established principles can be of greater benefit than a great deal of speech which simply rambles on, and through hearing you don't actually receive very much benefit from.

This is the reality which is present in our time; one sees a tremendous amount of speech which only possesses within it a small amount of actual knowledge. We see the presence of many speakers yet few people of true understanding and comprehension.' "

[The eminent major scholar Sheikh Saaleh al-Fauzaan, may Allaah preserve him- 'A Valued Gift for the Reader Of Comments Upon the Book Sharh as-Sunnah', page 102-103]

This pocket edition is based upon appendixes taken from the larger book:

The Cure, The Explanation, The Clear Affair, & The Brilliantly Distinct Signpost:

Book 1: Sources of Islaam & The Way of the Companions

Based upon
'Usul as-Sunnah' of Imaam Ahmad
(may Allaah have mercy upon him)

The original course book, is part of a full series, intended to be a vital learning tool, by Allaah's persmission, for discussing and learning many of the most important sources of Islaam, how to implement them, and how to avoid common mistakes and misunderstandings.

This full course series is based upon various commentaries of the original text, from the following scholars of our age, may Allaah have mercy upon then or preserve them:

Sheikh Zayd Ibn Muhammad al-Madkhalee
Sheikh Saleeh Ibn Sa'd As-Suhaaymee
Sheikh 'Abdul-'Azeez Ibn 'Abdullah ar-Raajhee
Sheikh Rabee'a Ibn Haadee al-Madkhalee
Sheikh Sa'd Ibn Naasir as-Shathree
Sheikh 'Ubayd Ibn 'Abdullah al-Jaabiree
Sheikh 'Abdullah al-Bukharee
Sheikh Hamd al-'Uthmaan…and other scholars

Each course book lesson has: lesson text, scholastic commentary, evidence summary, lesson benefits, standard & review exercises, as well as the Arabic text & translation of 'Usul as-Sunnah' in Arabic divided for easier memorization.

Compiled and Translated by:
Abu Sukhailah Khalil Ibn-Abelahyi

[Available: **Now**, pages: **470+**
price: (Soft cover) **$30**
(Hard cover) **$45**
(Kindle) **$9.99**]

LET THE SCHOLARS SPEAK- CLARITY & GUIDANCE (BOOK 1)

DISTINGUISHING THE TRUTH & IT'S PEOPLE: KNOWLEDGE, INTELLECT & THE JAMAA'AH

Translated & Compiled By
Abu Sukhailah Khalil Ibn-Abelahyi

Table of Contents

Amended Introduction *10*

The Criterion for Distinguishing the Truth an Individual Must Follow *122*

Important Advice Towards Adhering Firmly to the Book of Allaah and the Pure Sunnah *126*

Three Questions on Acquiring Knowledge, Recognizing True Scholars, and the Meaning of Methodology *132*

Considering The Scholar Of The Sunnah Your Sheikh Due To Having Listened To His Lectures & Having Read His Books *138*

Know Whom You Are Taking Your Religion From! *144*

THe Correct Meaning of Adhering to the Jamaa'ah *152*

Choose Good Companions Oh Men and Women of the Sunnah!. *160*

Signposts for the Use Or Abuse of the Intellect in Islaam.............. *170*

The Position Of Abu Bakr & 'Umar With The Messenger Of Allaah . *180*

AMENDED INTRODUCTION

In the name of Allaah, The Most Gracious, The Most Merciful
Verily, all praise is due to Allaah, we praise Him, we seek His assistance and we ask for His forgiveness. We seek refuge in Him from the evils of our souls and the evils of our actions. Whoever Allaah guides, no one can lead him astray and whoever is caused to go astray, there is no one that can guide him. I bear witness that there is no deity worthy of worship except Allaah alone with no partners. And I bear witness that Muhammad is His worshipper and Messenger.

Oh you who believe, fear Allaah as He ought to be feared and do not die except while you are Muslims. -(Surah Aal-'Imraan:102)

Oh mankind, fear Allaah who created you from a single soul and from that, He created its mate. And from them He brought forth many men and women. And fear Allaah to whom you demand your mutual rights. Verily, Allaah is an ever All-Watcher over you. -(Surah an-Nisaa:1)

Oh you who believe, fear Allaah and speak a word that is truthful (and to the point) - He will rectify your deeds and forgive you your sins. And whoever obeys Allaah and His Messenger has achieved a great success. -(Surah al-Ahzaab:70-71)

As for what follows:

THE SUCCESS OF MUSLIMS IS FOUNDED UPON AUTHENTIC BELIEFS AND ACTIONS UPON THEM

The guiding scholar Sheikh Muhammad Ibn Saaleh al-'Utheimeen, may Allaah, the Most High, have mercy upon him, was asked,[1] **"What would be the effects and consequences, upon the current condition of the Muslim Ummah, of sound efforts to call Muslims to having the correct beliefs, and the sound methodology of Islaam?"** He answered,

> *There is no doubt that the effect of calling people to have the correct beliefs and the correct methodology upon the life of the Muslim Ummah would be something significant and substantial. This effect was shown and manifested in the lives of the Companions of the Messenger of Allaah, may Allaah be pleased with them all, in the other two distinguished early generations, and within the lives of all those Muslims who followed them in goodness. It is seen in their honor and prominence, in their having satisfied good lives both in the world and eventually in the next....*
>
> *...If the people rectify their beliefs, and establish upon those true beliefs their rulings and judgements in the general matters of life, with the Muslims, as a whole, adopting and truly embracing what is correct and sound, then they will undoubtedly achieve what those early Muslims from the first generations, who proceeded them, achieved of honor, prestige, and lives of contentment.*
>
> *Just as if they fail to embrace the correct beliefs, and act upon them, then they will end up in the same lowly state that the rest of humanity finds itself in. And Allaah the Most High, knows best.*

There is no doubt that we as Muslims, are those who love

[1] Majmua' al-Fatawaa wa Rasi'al Fadheelatul-Sheikh Muhammad Ibn Saaleh al-'Utheimeen: vol. 27 pg. 44-46

Islaam and are those who want good for our Ummah, the people of Islaam. For this reason we should ask ourselves, what was the way which the first generations of Muslims understood and practiced Islaam that made them successful- enabling them to bring good to themselves and others by the mercy of Allaah, who has among His names al-Fattah, the Opener? How did they *"embrace the correct beliefs, and act upon them"*, meaning both the general Muslims and those incredible early scholars, in a way that brought them success? As indeed, the scholars generally among the Muslims have always played a central role in their well being and success. In clarifying exactly who we are speaking about when referring to their correct understanding and practice, Sheikh Hammaad Ibn Muhammad al-Ansaaree, may Allaah have mercy upon him, said,[2]

> *"Whenever the scholars use the expression "the early scholars said..." What is intended by this are those scholars who lived before the fourth century according to the hijree calendar. These first three centuries after the time of Messenger are the centuries of the scholars who are the Salaf. Since after the fourth century, divisions and separation began."*

There was a clear methodology of Islaam during the early generations, that both brought them unity and lead them to true success in times of both difficulty and ease. In giving important detail as to how they, the first Muslim generations, proceeded in realizing Allaah's religion, Sheikh Saaleh Aal-Sheikh, may Allaah preserve him, said, [3]

> *....we know that the beliefs of the righteous first three generations and their methodology is only a single way and path which it is obligatory that we ourselves follow*

---

[2] Al-Majmu'a from the Biography of Sheikh Hammaad Ibn Muhammad al-Ansaaree: Number 77
[3] From the lecture "Provisions in the Study of Fundamental Beliefs and Methodology"

and adhere to. It is that affair, which encompasses within it, that leads to the success of the people. Because the Prophet, may the praise and salutations of Allaah be upon him, explained clearly that this Muslim Ummah would separate into seventy three different sects. And he, may the praise and salutations of Allaah be upon him, said, {...All of them are in the Hellfire except for one. That is the 'Jamaa'ah'.} And in the wording of another narration the Companions asked him, "Who are they, oh Messenger of Allaah?" He replied: {Those who are upon what I and my Companions are upon.}

This indicates that the correct methodology and the correct fundamental beliefs are that single path and way of the Muslims who adhere to the Jamaa'ah, meaning the way of the Companions, the original way of the first three righteous generations. Additionally, it is well known that the way of the Companions of the Messenger of Allaah, may Allaah be pleased with them all, in beliefs and in methodology was a single clear distinct way.

Therefore true success, can only be found through these practices of theirs which they followed. Just as how this methodology was that which rectified the first generations, likewise it will also bring success to the later generations. Just as it was what brought success to the first part of this Muslim Ummah, likewise it is the only thing which is suited and capable of bringing success to the latter part or later generations of the Muslim Ummah. This is due to several reasons, including those specific merits and distinguishing features of this methodology proceeded upon by the Companions.

Even though some Muslims do not realize the importance of striving upon that original methodology, Sheikh Saaleh Ibn Fauzaan, may Allaah preserve him, explains that the need for it is even greater now,[4]

> "As the later periods of time approach, the strangeness of Islaam will increase, and the trials which the believers face become more common and severe, such that the Muslims will need to have even greater concern to adhering to the methodology of the Salaf of this Ummah."

Imaam 'Abdul-'Azeez Ibn Baaz, may Allaah have mercy upon him, explained in his well known collection of Islamic rulings, how important it is for us to recognize that any true rectification of our current condition must be connected to that first rectification Islaam brought,[5]

> "The one who wishes to rectify Islamic society, and to rectify other societies and nations by other than the path and the means and methods by which the first Islamic society was put aright has fallen into error, and spoken with other than the truth."

Sheikh Saaleh Ibn Fauzaan, may Allaah preserve him, explained to us that this same understanding is key, not only for rectification but also to stop us from straying from Allaah's guidance overall, [6]

> "If Muslims do not properly understand the way of the first generations of Muslims, and we are deficient in our knowledge of it, without studying, then undoubtedly those Muslims, lacking understanding, will go astray and become misguided."

He, may Allaah preserve him, also clarified to us that this key understanding has teeth which enable it to turn and open the door of success for Muslims,[7]

> "It is not possible that we can understand the way of

---

[4] The True Need Of The Muslim Ummah Of Following The Way Of The First Three Generations. pg. 13
[5] Majmua' Fataawa wa Maqallat: vol: 1 pg. 249
[6] The True Need Of The Muslim Ummah Of Following The Way Of The First Three Generations. pg. 11-12
[7] The True Need Of The Muslim Ummah Of Following The Way Of The First Three Generations. pg. 12

the first three generations except after having studied it, and worked to learn it, by studying it and teaching it to others along with our continuing to ask Allaah ❴ **Guide us to the straight path.** ❵

He also, may Allaah preserve him, additionally reminded us of the importance of proceeding with patience in our sincere efforts for Islaam, towards gradual success of our Ummah, after having gained sound authentic knowledge of the way of the first Muslims,[8]

> *"You will not be firmly established upon the way of the first three generations except after striving to understand it and having learned about it. And you will not have adhered to it properly except after striving to proceed patiently upon it."*

This advice echoes what Imaam Ahmad Ibn Hanbal, may Allaah have mercy upon him, said,[9]

> *"May Allaah have mercy upon that worshiper who speaks with the truth, adheres to those transmitted reports of guidance, holds firmly to the Sunnah, and closely follows the way of the righteous Muslims."*

We should earnestly ask, do most Muslims have sufficient knowledge of that clear methodology our beloved Prophet stood firmly upon and proceeded upon? Do we understand how he personally understood and then guided his family to understand the clear beliefs and practices of Islaam? Do we know what his guidance was in dealing with others, whether neighbors or other nations? Do we understand how his Companions followed him in all these important matters of implementing Islaam? If we do not have that clear firm general knowledge of his beautiful guiding way of life, his methodology, based upon the proofs and evidences which our scholars throughout

---

[8] The True Need Of The Muslim Ummah Of Following The Way Of The First Three Generations. pg. 13
[9] Tabaqaat al-Hanaabilah: vol. 1 pg. 36

the centuries have preserved for us and explained, how could we possibly work towards rectifying ourselves and our families as previous generations successfully did?

Sheikh Ibn Baaz, may Allaah have mercy upon him, also reminds us with an essential reminder of the incredible value and importance of having sound knowledge about Islaam,[10]

> *"The gaining of Sharee'ah knowledge is from the most excellent types of provision someone can be blessed with. It is takes someone from the restrictive tightness of ignorance and its dark shadow, into the breadth and expansiveness of revealed knowledge and its light."*

From the leading scholars of our age, who was responsible for helping spread authentic Sharee'ah to his own land and around the world, was Sheikh Muqbil Ibn Haadee al-Waadi'ee, may Allaah have abundant mercy upon him. His students are spread throughout Yemen, and those who benefited from his efforts directly and indirectly are spread around the world. Sheikh Muqbil ibn Haadee al-Waadi'ee, may Allaah have mercy upon him, similarly made clear that,[11]

> *"The most severe thing the Muslims have been afflicted with today is ignorance.."*

He, may Allaah have mercy upon him, also said,[12]

> *"If you were to learn and study, to the true degree of Muslims need for knowledge now, you would have to strive, night and day, in seeking knowledge."*

He, may Allaah have mercy upon him, encouraged us in spreading true knowledge of Islaam,[13]

> *"Be diligent in teaching the Muslims and working to increase their understanding of Islaam."*

---

[10] Majmua' Fataawa wa Maqallat: vol: 1 pg. 350
[11] Al-Bashaa'ir Fe as-Samaa'a al-Mubashir by 'Abdullah Ibn Ayyash al-Ahdal: pg 22
[12] Al-Bashaa'ir Fe as-Samaa'a al-Mubashir by 'Abdullah Ibn Ayyash al-Ahdal: pg 23
[13] Al-Bashaa'ir Fe as-Samaa'a al-Mubashir by 'Abdullah Ibn Ayyash al-Ahdal: pg 13

To those Muslims coming to Yemen from outside countries who traveled for knowledge he said,[14]

> "If you learn and gain knowledge in order to return and teach the people of your land, this is better for you than if you returned back to them carrying a basket filled with gold."

And he, may Allaah have mercy upon him, advised them about what they teach saying,[15]

> "If you go back to your country then teach the Qur'aan, as well as shorter hadeeth narrations. I advise every such brother to teach the people with that knowledge he has acquired which is basic and simple in nature."

Sheikh Muqbil ibn Haadee al-Waadi'ee, may Allaah have mercy upon him, also explained that we should help remove false ideas and incorrect interpretations wherever we live,[16]

> "O people of the Sunnah, the society is in your care and custody. You are responsible for refuting the misguidance of the Raafidhee as well as refuting every clear opposer to the guidance of Islaam."

He, may Allaah have mercy upon him, explained the importance of remembering that,[17]

> "The Sunnah did not spread except through the efforts of those who were resolute and steadfast upon it, and who did not compromise and accept innovations as part of Islaam."

---

[14] Al-Bashaa'ir Fe as-Samaa'a al-Mubashir by 'Abdullah Ibn Ayyash al-Ahdal: pg 13
[15] Al-Bashaa'ir Fe as-Samaa'a al-Mubashir by 'Abdullah Ibn Ayyash al-Ahdal: pg 18
[16] Al-Bashaa'ir Fe as-Samaa'a al-Mubashir by 'Abdullah Ibn Ayyash al-Ahdal: pg 14
[17] Al-Bashaa'ir Fe as-Samaa'a al-Mubashir by 'Abdullah Ibn Ayyash al-Ahdal: pg 28

He mentioned the importance of countering foreign concepts that began to take root in some Muslim lands,[18]

> *"I advise you to compete and surpass the efforts of the advocates of secularism and those calling to Communism."*

Similarly, he encouraged us to convey the true guidance of Islaam to the general people before others reached them with something which was misguidance, [19]

> *"Oh people of the Sunnah, reach the general people before the people of falsehood do, in order to defend and protect our religion."*

These last two advices remind us that we should also be generally aware of those who work against the Muslim Ummah generally, and have always put forth determined efforts to weaken and reduce the vital connection of the Muslims to guiding light of authentic Sharee'ah knowledge. This begins with Shaytaan as Ibn Jawzee, may Allaah have mercy upon him, said,[20]

> *"Know that the first deception of Iblees upon humanity was preventing them from gaining knowledge. Because knowledge is light, if he is able to put out their lamps of guidance, then he can direct them into the darkness in any way he wishes."*

Our scholars, all praise is due to Allaah, explain and publicly clarify how this occurs in our present age. They explain that this opposition is encountered from the direction of the enemies from outside the Muslim Ummah, as Sheikh Hammaad Ibn Muhammad al-Ansaaree, may Allaah have mercy upon him, explained,[21]

> *"Whenever Europe was able to dominate or conquer*

---

[18] Al-Bashaa'ir Fe as-Samaa'a al-Mubashir by 'Abdullah Ibn Ayyash al-Ahdal: pg 15
[19] Al-Bashaa'ir Fe as-Samaa'a al-Mubashir by 'Abdullah Ibn Ayyash al-Ahdal: pg 15
[20] Talbees Iblees of Ibn Jawzee, vol. 3 pg. 389
[21] Al-Majmu'a from the Biography of Sheikh Hammaad Ibn Muhammad al-Ansaaree: Number 139

> *any land from the Muslim countries, they endeavored to steal and carry way the sources of that countries' Islamic heritage from the original classical manuscripts and writings of the scholars, and similar sources of Sharee'ah knowledge. As they understand the importance of those sources of this religious heritage."*

There is no doubt that weakening our connection to authentic Sharee'ah knowledge enabled them to strive to spread disunity among Muslims. Sheikh Saaleh Ibn Fauzaan, may Allaah preserve him, also said,[22]

> *"It is not in fact strange, meaning what we live with and face today of threats and intimidation from the disbelievers, and their efforts to spread disunity among the Muslim Ummah..."*

Likewise this enmity is also encountered from the destructive efforts of those who were newly emerged enemies of the religion of Islaam generally from within the lands of the Muslims. He, Sheikh Hammaad, may Allaah have mercy upon him, explained this saying,[23]

> *"One of the things carried out by Jamaal 'Abdul-Naasir in Egypt during the time he was in power, was killing the most intelligent of the scholars who were present then. In a similar way this is comparable to what was done by Saddam Hussein in Iraq when he undertook to make sure he killed the most knowledgeable scholars present in that land (of Iraq)."*

He also reminded the Muslims that, additionally, there were also poisonous efforts, whose aim was to disconnect the Muslims from their connection to the first three generations and the sunnah of the rightly guided khaleefahs, coming from those people of innovation in

---

[22] The Correct Position of a Muslim Towards Trials, Societal demonstrations, and Political Revolutions: pg 11
[23] Al-Majmu'a from the Biography of Sheikh Hammaad Ibn Muhammad al-Ansaaree: Number 22

the religion who falsely claim to love to the Sunnah- but in beliefs and practices placed the innovation far ahead of it,[24]

> *"There aren't any parties who print and publish books that oppose the call to the way of the Salaf in the world, like has been done by previous authorities in Turkey, and now by the government of the Raafidhah in Iran.*
>
> *Indeed the spread of the beliefs of Salafeeyah did not start to diminish in acceptance historically until the power of the Turkish Empire, as among their ranks were the Naqshabandeeyah Sufees. The Naqshabandeeyah are clear enemies of the beliefs of those who follow the first three generations of Muslims."*

So we should not foolishly believe that there are not those continually working to separate us from properly learning and practicing our religion. The guiding scholar Sheikh al-'Utheimeen, may Allaah, the Most High, have mercy upon him, was asked, "**What is the correct guided way to confront and oppose those who fight against our practicing Islaam?** He replied,[25]

> *" What is obligatory upon the Muslims is to oppose every attack or weapon directed against Islaam with that approach which is suitable and appropriate in confronting it:*
>
> *Those who fight against Islaam and the Muslims intellectually with misguided concepts and deceptive statements then it is obligatory that we explain the falsehood they contain by putting forth sound intellectual arguments which are used along with the correct Sharee'ah proofs and evidences.*

---

[24] Al-Majmu'a from the Biography of Sheikh Hammaad Ibn Muhammad al-Ansaaree: Number 64
[25] Majmua al-Fatawaa wa rasia'l Fadheelatul-Sheikh Muhammad Ibn Saaleh al-'Utheimeen: vol. 27 pg. 43-439

Those who fight against Islaam and the Muslims from the aspect of economic pressure and similar campaigns, it is obligatory that we block such campaigns, and in fact that we direct back toward them similar campaigns to those which they used to economically attack the Muslims, and make clear to them that the best way to establish economic relations is upon equity and fairness, which is what Islaam itself establishes.

Those who fight against Islaam and the Muslim nations with military weapons, then it is obligatory that we oppose this with similar forces equipped to oppose those military attacks against us. It is for this reason that Allaah, the Most High says, ❰ **O Prophet! Strive hard against the disbelievers and the hypocrites, and be severe against them; their abode will be Hell, – and worst indeed is that destination.** ❱ *–(Surah at-Tahreem: 09).*

Additionally, regarding this it is well known that the fighting in Allaah's path against those who are hypocrites is not conducted in the same manner as against those disbelievers who physically attack Muslims. As the struggle against the hypocrites assaulting Islaam is conducted with knowledge and explanations, whereas the struggle again the disbelievers who physically and militarily attack Muslims, is undertaken with comparable weapons and armaments."

Yet despite the attacks against Islaam from internal and external opponents, Allaah has not only protected our incredible legacy of authentic knowledge from the Salaf and those in every century who followed them, but in fact caused it to spread further across the world today. This is something we should be incredibly thankful for, and certainly shukr or thankfulness is a form of inward worship. Continually, day after day, decade after decade, the call to turn back and look carefully at that original Islaam that our beloved Prophet placed firmly in the hands of his noble Companions, gains more and more acceptance throughout the Muslim Ummah, despite the hatred which both the disbelievers and the people of innovation have for this.

Undoubtedly, the sound and authentic knowledge of Islaam is one of the most valuable tools we have as Muslims. As both individuals and families, we should not shy away from bringing the tremendously valuable heritage and life spring of authentic knowledge into our personal and family lives, no matters what stage we find ourselves in today individually. Even if we just embraced Islaam yesterday, authentic Sharee'ah knowledge is a incredible blessing that always strengthens our connection to the guided Muslims, in every century, who proceeded us, in both understanding and practice. For this reason, there is glad tiding for every sincere striving Muslim who says, "*I follow that religion which the Prophet taught to Abu Bakr and 'Umar.*"[26]

We believe that as Imaam Ibn Hajr al-Asqalaanee, may Allaah have mercy upon him, said,[27]

> *"Just as rain brings life back to the dry land which has died, so do the branches of the Sharee'ah knowledge give life to those hearts which have died."*

---

[26] A reference to the narration *{Follow those who succeed me: Abu Bakr and 'Umar.}* as authenticated by Sheikh al-Albaanee in as-Silsilah al-Hadeeth as-Saheehah: Narration 1233

[27] Fath al-Baaree Sharh Saheeh al-Bukhaaree: vol. 1 pg. 177

Understanding What Knowledge in Islaam You as an Individual Must Study

For some Muslims, even after recognizing its importance, the undertaking of increasing their knowledge of Islaam may at first seem overwhelming and too much of a burden when added to the other responsibilities they shoulder everyday. However, without question, sound Sharee'ah knowledge was an essential foundation that enabled that rectification of the very first society which Muslims found themselves within.[28] They undertook both learning it and living it despite being busy with their wives, children, and livelihoods, just as we are. If we also want that same success they were blessed with, we must walk the same path they walked upon. Without authentic knowledge as our foundation, our success is not possible in this world nor the next. We must remind ourselves, and each other, of the real indispensable value study of Islaam holds for us, as Sheikh Ibn Baaz, may Allaah have mercy upon him, stated, [29]

> *"Gaining beneficial knowledge is from the most significant of matters that facilitate your affairs and makes things easier. Because the one seeking and learning Sharee'ah knowledge comes to understand through his knowledge the different aspects of what is good and the reasons and causes of reaching success in his life, which is not something easy for the one who is ignorant."*

From the early scholars Ibn Shehaab, may Allaah have mercy upon him, said,[30]

> *"Just as one cannot have printing without letters, likewise one cannot gain knowledge without seeking,*

---

[28] The intent here are those Muslims who embraced Islaam after the coming of the final prophet and messenger. As without question the true followers of every prophet and messenger and their original revealed guidance were all considered Muslims in the general meaning of Islaam.
[29] Majmua' Fataawa wa Maqallat: vol: 1 pg. 350
[30] Jaame'a Bayaan al-'Ilm wa Fadhlihee: vol. 1 pg. 200

meaning the efforts needed to gain it."

One of the first steps upon the well worn path of guidance the Companions proceeded upon, is correctly understanding in detail what is specifically required from us as individuals, in terms of gaining Sharee'ah knowledge that we need inwardly and outwardly. This means understanding which aspects or areas of knowledge are obligatory upon each individual mature capable Muslim, without exception. These aspects, as a whole, form the understanding each of us needs to be able to properly worship Allaah alone as He has required from us. Sheikh Saaleh Aal-Sheikh, may Allaah preserve him, makes this clear,[31]

> *"It is not generally intended that every person who seeks knowledge should seek to eventually become a scholar, rather what is sought after in your seeking to acquire Sharee'ah knowledge is to remove that ignorance that you have, such that you are able to properly worship Allaah, the Most Glorified and the Most Exalted, through sound authentic expressions of true worship, that you come to have the sound authentic beliefs of Islaam, so that you are able to eventually reach Allaah, the Most Glorified and the Most Exalted, on the Day of Judgement with a clean heart.*
>
> *Allaah, the Most High, said,* ﴾ **The Day whereon neither wealth nor sons will avail. Except him who brings to Allaah a clean heart,** ﴿ *-(Surah ash-Shu'ara': 88-89). Here clean means free from false ideas and misconceptions, as well as free from the burden of wrongly following your base desires in the understanding and practice of the religion. This is the true benefit and fruit which comes from of gaining Sharee'ah knowledge, that you remove ignorance from yourself."*

---

[31] From the audio cassette Ten Advices On Benefiting From One's Lessons' by Sheikh Saaleh Aal-Sheikh

Many Muslims fail to recognize that, as the Sheikh mentioned above, one of the main aims of the obligation of gaining a degree of Sharee'ah knowledge is in order to free yourself *"from false ideas and misconceptions,"* as well as free ourselves from *"the burden of wrongly following your base desires in the understanding and practice of the religion."* There is often a concentration on learning and developing the ability to properly perform outward forms of worship, while unfortunately neglecting the development of the correct inward beliefs and understanding which are in fact the foundation for our outward deeds and endeavors. The correct methodology focuses upon both.

It is important to affirm as the scholars have indicated, that the boundaries of the individual obligation of knowledge should never be restricted to just outward deeds, such that we neglect developing the strong evidenced inward beliefs, and the essential inward actions of our hearts- such as loving and hating for the sake of Allaah,[32] along with the authentic outward acts of authentic worship and practices that distinguish Islaam, as a path of guidance.

The following related question was asked to the Permanent Committee For Scholastic Research and Issuing of Islamic Rulings, *"I'm a student in the college of medicine at al-Azhar University. I find that studying and reviewing for my classes and lectures at the college takes the majority of my time and significant effort on my part. So I have little opportunity to learn and study my religion as a Muslim. How can I make my efforts of studying and reviewing at college and my attending it something encompassing the worship of Allaah? Such that, in so*

---

[32] Despite the common practice of rejecting hate absolutely, which is an action of the heart, a righteous Muslim should hate whatever Allaah hates, such as practices of associating partners with Him in worship, the hating of which is essential to true Islaam. This is a matter of required inward worship of the heart which the Prophet taught and encouraged among the generation of the Companions, *{The Prophet said: The best of the actions is to love for the sake of Allaah and to hate for the sake of Allaah.}* as authentically narrated in Sunan Abu Dawud no. 4599, Imaam Ahmad in his Musnad no. 21696, and al-Bazaar in his Musnad no. 4076.

doing, Allaah may grant me good and blessings from him, and open up for me the doors of knowledge of Islaam from him, and enable me to be successful in this effort. This is in order that, I may be someone seeking knowledge who comes to benefit the Muslims, someone contributing to the might and force of Islaam. Please benefit us all with a comprehensive response to this, may Allaah reward you with good." They responded,[33]

> *"It is obligatory upon the Muslim that they learned those specific matters within their religion that enable them to properly perform and complete the various obligatory affairs in their religion. It is not permissible that they allow themselves to be preoccupied from gaining this obligatory knowledge. Similarly, the study of medicine is from those areas which is held to be a collective obligation upon the Muslims, whereas studying the religion of Islaam is actually an individual obligation, in respect to those areas of knowledge which are required for every single Muslim. As such, one's individual obligation must be given precedence over focusing upon something which is a collective obligation.*
>
> *For this reason, it is obligatory upon you that you learn the fundamental affairs of your religion, which are required for you to perform whatever is obligatory upon you. But fulfilling this does not prevent you from also studying medicine. Additionally, it is possible that you can make your efforts of learning the science of medicine, and your studying it, an act of worship, through establishing your sincerity in doing that for Allaah alone, and through your intention for it to be something which benefits both yourself and the Muslims generally,*
>
> *This would be through establishing efforts in the field of medicine, which fulfill the needs of the Muslims in*

---

[33] First Question from Ruling #8849 from Permanent Committee For Scholastic Reasearch and Issuing of Islamic Rulings

relation to maintaining their health, and preventing them from being stricken by different diseases, all by the permission of Allaah the Most Perfect and the Most High. In this way you can make your studies a form of worship, upon having this righteous intention.

And the success is from Allaah. May the salutations and praise of Allaah be upon our Prophet Muhammad, his family, and his Companions."

Sheikh Saaleh al-Fauzaan, clarifies further details of this distinction in his explanation of the 'Nullifiers of Islaam' by dividing the Sharee'ah knowledge we study into separate categories,[34]

"Learning knowledge of of two categories:

The first category: that knowledge which it is obligatory upon every single Muslim to learn, and which no one has an legitimate excuse for being ignorant about it. This is that understanding without which someone cannot be steadfast as a worshipper in his practice of Islaam, such as understanding of the correct essential beliefs and what opposes or nullifies them. Also understanding of the obligatory rulings related to the ritual prayers and zakaat, obligatory fasting, pilgrimage and 'umraah, by this meaning the five fundamental pillars of Islaam. It is required that every Muslim and Muslimah learn these matters. Otherwise, if they do not gain that knowledge related to these five pillars, how will they be able to practice their religion in the way which conforms to the revealed Sharee'ah?

The second category: that knowledge which learning it is a collective obligation of the Muslims jointly, but not an obligation upon every single Muslim individually. Rather, it is for those with the aptitude for learning it.

---

[34] Explanation of the Nullifiers of Islaam: pg. 189

This is studying the remaining areas of knowledge, from the fiqh of business dealings and interactions, laws of inheritance, marriage and divorce regulations, those criminal punishments implemented by the Muslim ruler, and other detailed areas of the knowledge of Islaam.

This level of knowledge is a collective obligation to be fulfilled according to the level of the people's need for those individuals who gain firm understanding in these areas. If it is learned by some of the Muslims to the extent that the Muslim's need is fulfilled as a whole, then the obligation of learning it is removed from the remaining Muslims. Yet, even when not an obligation, studying these additional areas, is relation to these other Muslims, is still generally considered a beneficial undertaking or endeavor which is from the best of established righteous endeavors. Yet since it is not easy for everyone to learn these more advanced areas of Sharee'ah knowledge, studying them is only a obligation upon the Muslims as a whole."

Once we understand both the importance of studying the knowledge of our religion generally, and properly undertake the specific scope of what is obligatory to learn individually, we also have the obligation to take the next step and seek opportunities to gradually influence and patiently guide and direct our own families towards understanding and proceeding, by our sides, upon the same path of gaining whatever knowledge is feasible, step by step. Sheikh Muhammad Ibn Saaleh al-'Utheimeen, may Allaah have mercy upon him, pointed out that this opportunity to guide our close family is something which should not be neglected,[35]

"None of you should be simply living with his family, yet like someone who is, in a way, absent by not enjoining and encouraging them towards what is good and from

[35] Adh-Dheeyaa' al-Laama' :156

guidance, as well as not forbidding and preventing them from wrongdoing and matters which are corrupting."

Similarly, Sheikh Saaleh Ibn al-Fauzaan, may Allaah preserve him, said,[36]

"Trials and corrupting tribulations are very severe at present, so do not be heedless and inattentive in terms of affair of your children and the women of your household."

It is also important that we realize that this obligation it is not a burden but a blessing. The results of which can only be good for us as an Ummah, but also importantly, individually. al-Quradhee, may Allaah have mercy upon him, said,[37]

"There is nothing that brings more delight and coolness to the eyes of a believer than seeing his wife and his children, obedient and striving to worship Allaah, the Most Glorified and the Most Exalted."

The gaining of this specific obligatory knowledge individually, and then cultivating the desire and efforts to gain it and use it within our families, is something we must give needed and consistent attention to. In this way, we are able to properly undertake seeking Sharee'ah knowledge individually and within our families, whenever that is possible, whereever we may be upon Allaah's earth. Along with that we should strive to remain as close as possible to the different reliable people of knowledge in order to guide our lives as Muslims generally. Sheikh Muhammad Baazmool, may Allaah preserve him, shows us this direct action plan, which the correct general methodology of Islaam offers, for the Muslim or Muslimah striving for the success of him or herself and their Muslim children. It also contributes greatly to making the Ummah successful

---

[36] From His Explanation of Ighaathatul al-Lahafaan min Masaa'id ash-Shaytaan given on 06-17-1437
[37] Tafseer al-Baghawee vol. 6 pg. 99

generally, as seen among the first Muslims,[38]

Do you want to bring victory to the Muslim Ummah? Do you wish to turn the schemes of the disbelievers back against them? Do you seek the raising up of the flag of the Sunnah and the elevation of its people, and to contribute to the weakening and waning of innovations wrongly attached to Islaam and those people upon it? If so, the way is something simple and easy, be diligent in implementing the Sunnah individually and realizing the guidance of the religion upon yourself, then by working similarly with those closest to you, and then continuing with those next to them in closeness.

In this way by Allaah's permission the Muslim Ummah will gradually start to fully implement Islaam, and the people of the Sunnah will find success of establishment throughout the earth. As Allaah has said, **Allaah has promised those among you who believe and do righteous good deeds, that He will certainly grant them succession to the present rulers in the land, as He granted it to those before them, and that He will grant them the authority to practice their religion which He has chosen for them. And He will surely give them in exchange a safe security after their fear provided they worship Me and do not associate anything in worship with Me. But whoever disbelieved after this, they are the rebellious, disobedient to Allaah.** *-(Surah an-Nur: 55)*

This matter is in reality at its heart simple, and the first path to take in achieving it is seeking to acquire Sharee'ah knowledge which is built firmly from the Book of Allaah and the Sunnah, upon the understanding the Salaf had of them both. Then to act upon this and implement it upon yourself initially. Thereafter start to call other people toward this way, staring with those

---
[38] From the Facebook page of Sheikh Muhammad Ibn 'Umar Baazmool 11-28-17 Various Statements 1329

*closest to you, and then afterwards with those next in closeness, and proceed in all these stages with patience. As Allaah says, "**By al-'Asr (the time). Verily, man is in loss, Except those who believe and do righteous good deeds, and recommend one another to the truth, and recommend one another to patience.**"*

Do not become dismayed or intimidated,...... as victory is coming....Since falsehood was present for a time, but the truth will become manifest for an enduring period!

Also it is important to not become discouraged by difficulties or setbacks or overwhelmed by the challenge, instead persevere upon sincerity, always making supplications for your eventual full success. Many of your brothers and sisters who started out having difficulty in learning and studying eventually came to not only gain a good understanding, but eventually excelled in the knowledge of Islaam. Sheikh Muhammad Ibn 'Umar Baazmool, may Allaah preserve him, recalls his own experience saying,[39]

> *"I recall that in the beginning of my committing myself to acquiring knowledge that I read a book from cover to cover, but I had only understood from it five percent of what it contained and nothing more.*
>
> *And I also recall that there was an occasion where I went and visited one of my close associates, and he was from those people who were educated, may Allaah have mercy upon him. I said to him, "There are a number of things that I don't understand in the book of so-and-so! So he said, "Bring it to me, and I will try to explain it to you."*
>
> *When I brought the book to him, he looked at it and saw that on some of the pages, I had underlined one or two lines on some of the pages, and that on others I had*

---
[39] From the facebook of the Sheikh April 26, 2018

not underlined anything from the pages' lines at all.

So he asked me, "Are the lines you have underlined, what you're having a problem understanding?" I replied, "No, those are the only parts which I truly understood!"

I also recall another occasion in the early days of my seeking knowledge, when I was sitting with some of my brothers. They were discussing the issue of the details of how the one performing the ritual prayer should go down into the position of prostration.

The question was should he go down on his two hands first, or down upon his knees first? One of them said to me, "Haven't you read the statement of ash-Shawkaanee in his work Nayl al-'Awtaar"? I replied, "I did read it fully, but I couldn't clearly discern what he considered the correct position in this issue!"

For this reason, my brother, the one who is a beginning seeker of knowledge should not lose hope and not become discouraged, nor be someone who is hasty. But instead proceed consistently, by continuing to read, reviewing whatever you are studying with your brothers, and listing to the statements of the people of knowledge.

Ensure that your intention is pure and sincerely for Allaah alone, then Allaah will facilitate matters and make things easy for you, by his permission. As this matter, just as was mentioned by the Messenger of Allaah, may Allaah's praise and salutations be upon him, said, **{Knowledge is gained through learning and forbearance is gained through enduring situations that force one to develop it, and whoever searches out good will be given it and whoever is wary of falling into evil, he will be protected from it.}**

For this reason, if you read a book and only understand five percent of it, but then read a second time and come to understand an additional five percent, then you have now doubled your understanding, and understood ten percent of that work. The amount that you will eventually understand from it will increase as long as you continue studying and striving, until you, by Allaah's permission, reach the level of actually understanding it well.

And perhaps there will come a time, that you will eventually recognize, that you have an inclination towards this area of knowledge you studied, and that you have managed to gain good comprehension within it. Then you must concentrate upon it, and increase your understanding within it, focusing on better learning it, until eventually you will excel by Allaah's permission."

We should realize that the way to help ourselves, and the Muslims generally, is clear and is not difficult to take the first steps upon. Yet once we understand the boundaries of that clear path we have recognized and turned towards, we must struggle daily to keep our feet planted firmly on it while relying upon Allaah for success in moving forward steadfastly. Furthermore, understanding that this struggle to learn and live Islaam correctly will not always be easy is something very important to recognize before encountering those difficulties and tests. As we will inevitably run up against these challenges as individuals, as Muslim families, as Muslim communities, and as the best Ummah raised among mankind. The guiding scholar Sheikh Saaleh Ibn Fauzaan, may Allaah preserve him, offers a warning and important reminder in saying,[40]

"There is always the danger of going astray, therefore is is required and necessary for every believer to stand steadfastly upon his religion, and be patient with difficulties, especially during the latter ages, in which

---

[40] Explanation of the book al-Kaba'ir pg. 557

> *there are present many different trials and tribulations which are encountered."*

Similarly, may Allaah preserve him, he also said,[41]

> *"Standing firmly upon the Sunnah is not an easy task, doing so always includes facing difficult tests and various trials. As there are people who will harass you, harm you, belittle and disparage you, saying about you, [This person is extreme and overly strict.] and similar descriptions.*
>
> *Moreover, perhaps that will not merely stop at harmful speech, but they may fight against you and physically assault you, or possibly imprison you. But, if you truly want success, remain patient regardless."*

There is an ever present need of a Muslim to ask, seek, and struggle towards being blessed by Allaah with steadfastness upon Islaam, after they have committed themselves to proceed upon the straight path of Islaam. The well known commentator of the Qur'aan al-Haafidh Ibn Katheer, may Allaah have mercy upon him, said,[42]

> *"Indeed a worshipper of Allaah is constantly in every hour and situation in true need of Allaah, the Most High blessing him with steadfastness upon His guidance."*

Sheikh 'Abdur-Razzaq al-Badr, may Allaah preserve him, said,[43]

> *"The worshiper of Allaah can not afford to be without the protection and support of his Lord even for a single moment. This is in order that he, the worshipper, remain protected, sufficed, secure, and guided as a Muslim. For this reason, it is legislated for the Muslim that each time he leaves his residence he says the supplication, "In the name of Allaah, I trust and rely upon Allaah, there is no*

---

[41] From his explanation of ad-Durrah al-Madheyah page, 190
[42] Tafseer Ibn Katheer: vol. 1 pg. 139
[43] Fiqh of Allaah's Beautiful Names, pg. 235

strength nor power except in Allaah."

In this way he is sufficed by this supplication while pursuing his needs and focusing on those things important to him, meaning that he is protected from falling into matters of harm, evil, or disease, and that he also be safeguarded against the danger of his enemies assaulting him, or him being struck by the oppression of those who oppress the people.

Sheikh Muhammad Ibn 'Umar Baazmool, may Allaah preserve him, stated the importance in always remembering that guidance to, and steadfastness upon, Islaam has always been the way of success the methodology of all the prophets and messengers, [44]

"As for steadfastness upon the religion, then the general counsel and directives which the prophets gave to the people is found in the statement of Allaah, the Most High, ❖ **And this (submission to Allaah, Islaam) was enjoined by 'Ibraaheem upon his sons and by Ya'qoob, saying, "O my sons! Allaah has chosen for you the true religion, then die not except in the Faith of Islaam (as Muslims).** ❖ *-(Surah al-Baqarah: 132)*

This is guidance to the straight path of Islaam, which Allaah has taught us to ask for it from Him within our supplications in our performance of ritual prayers. Indeed the Messenger of Allaah, may Allaah's praise and salutations be upon him, informed us, **[There is no prayer for the one who does not recite al-Faatihah from the Book of Allaah.]**, *and in this essential surah, Surah al-Faatihah, we recite the verse* ❖ **Guide us to the Straight Way** ❖ *-(Surah al-Faatihah: 6)*

Guidance is of three types or categories,

---

[44] Steadfastness upon the Methodology of the First Generations". of the Sheikh Muhammad Ibn 'Umar Baazmool: pg. 10

- *firstly being guided to understand and be aware of the truth,*

- *secondly guidance to properly affirm and truly accept the truth, after being guided to understand it, and*

- *thirdly the guidance of steadfastness in proceeding upon and living the truth and walking Allaah's straight path.*

Every time a worshiper of Allaah stops and turns to perform the ritual prayer, he is acknowledging that he needs each of these different types of guidance from his Lord."

Sheikh al-'Utheimeen, may Allaah have mercy upon him, discussed how this is also connected to turning, trusting, and relying upon Allaah in his explanation of the following verse,

❖ **None has the right to be worshipped but He, to Him is the final return.** ❖ *-(Surah Ghaafir: 3)*

From the benefits that can be derived from this noble verse is an encouragement to trust and rely upon Allaah. It may be asked how can this verse be an evidence for encouraging reliance upon Allaah? This is since whenever someone returns or comes back to Allaah, it is required that he be connected to Allaah alone and not anyone else. As long as someone must return back to Allaah, then he must have trust and reliance upon Allaah and not rely upon anyone else.

From the benefits that can be derived from this noble verse also is that one should take refuge and seeks the protection of Allaah during difficulties generally, and also whenever seeking something which you want in life. As that protection of fulfilment of the need, can only be taken from who? It can only be from the one to whom ❖ *...is the final return* ❖*. As such, whenever you* *encounter some hardship or difficult situation, do not complain about it to this one and that one, rather, it is upon you to bring it to Allaah, the Most Glorified and the Most Exalted.*

This includes those trials and tests that have indirect or less apparent causes or reasons, such that in attempting to rectify them no one will be able to truly help you other than Allaah. Indeed, Allaah says, ﴿ ***And if an evil whisper from Shaytaan (Satan) tries to turn you away (O Muhammad) (from doing good, etc.), then seek refuge in Allaah. Verily, He is the All-Hearer, the All-Knower.*** ﴾ *-(Surah Fussilat: 36)"*

One of the important ways to steadily grow and then remain steadfast upon Islaam is constantly assessing where we currently stand and the state of our personal practice of our religion at present. This requires honesty about deficiencies large and small in our individual knowledge, our priorities and focus, as well as our deeds and actions. Ibn al-Qayyim, may Allaah have mercy upon him, spoke about failing to engage in this self-assessment and the harm that comes from failing to recognize the priority it should have for every worshipper of Allaah, saying, [45]

"It is not for the one who is an adult and someone responsible to fall into heedlessness, turning away from self examination and calling himself to account, by simply letting oneself act in any manner, and being lax in important matters and simply going where they might be led. Acting this way only leads to your own ruin.

Moreover, this is the way of the people who are arrogant -they shut their eyes to their faults and wrongs, since they expect and rely on eventually being excused and forgiven. Therefore they neglect calling themselves to account and looking at their own faults and shortcomings.

---
[45] Ighaathatul-Lahfaan: vol. 1 pg. 136

Additionally, if such a person actually turns to examine himself, often he is still not bothered by his sins which he recognizes, as he has become accustomed to and numbingly comfortable with them, such that weaning and pulling himself away from them is something now quite difficult."

The result of neglecting this essential self accounting is that we find that many people often have not correctly established their relationship with the sole Creator and Sustainer, in the way which He has clearly commanded in the Qur'aan. Many times this problem or failure returns back to our lacking correct knowledge and understanding of who our Lord is and what He has commanded us to do in this life. Yet in every case this lapse or failure to hold ourselves to account, leads to many negative results in this world as well as, ultimately, in the next as Ibn al-Qayyim insightfully explains to us,[46]

"If you examine and consider you will find the case is that of the majority of the people you find simply focus upon their own rights from Allaah, and not those rights of Allaah that are due upon them to fulfill as His created worshippers.

From this misguided emphasis is produced a distance and disconnection from Allaah, from it comes the causing of their hearts to be shielded from properly comprehending Him as intended, and from it comes being shielded from fully loving him and desiring to meet Him, and from it comes being disconnected from gaining comfort and ease which is found in His remembrance.

This condition is the worst of the extremes of ignorance that a person may be afflicted with, meaning ignorance of both his Lord and of himself".

---

[46] From his work "Aid for the Yearning One in Resisting the Attacks of Shaytaan, vol. 1 pg. 88

Similarly, many people have often also not correctly established their relationships among Allaah's creation in a way which is correct according to revealed guidance, nor established their relationships in that proper way which would ultimately contribute to their success in the Hereafter. The leading scholar among the young Companions of the Messenger of Allaah - Ibn 'Abbaas, may Allaah be pleased with him, said,[47]

> *"The people today generally have based their relationships and essential associations upon some matter only connected to this worldly life, yet, eventually, the one who has done so will not be benefited by that with anything at all. Then he recited the verse,* ❀ **Friends on that Day will be foes one to another except the pious, those with taqwaa**❀-*(Surah az-Zukhruf:76)* .
>
> *And then he recited* ❀ **You (O Muhammad) will not find any people who believe in Allaah and the Last Day, making friendship with those who oppose Allaah and His Messenger...**❀-*(Surah al-Mujaadilah: 22)."*

We ask Allaah to bless us as Muslims, with true steadfastness in standing upon what He loves and is pleased with, in both our relationship with Him as our Lord, and in our relationships with His creation.

---

[47] al-Adaab ash-Sharee'ah of Ibn Muflih

THE RELIGION OF THE CHOSEN MESSENGER WAS BOTH BELIEF AND METHODOLOGY

In considering how the first generations truly established the worship of Allaah alone, and remained connected to guidance, we see that it was by remaining connected to the believers' way of Companions, as those who first believed in, practiced, and preserved that perfect revealed guidance of Islaam they received from the final prophet. By understanding this, we can then also recognize those Muslims who have failed to fully do so, regardless of whether that was intentionally or unintentionally. Some of them, who intentionally follow another newer methodology, and are stubborn in their opposition the way of the Salaf, will attack both the scholars and common Muslims adhering to the way of the first three generations. Sheikh Saaleh Ibn Fauzaan, may Allaah preserve him, said,[48]

"Hold fast to acting with patience as long you are convinced and sure that you stand upon the truth, do not turn your face to give consideration to the one who has been prevented from accepting the truth, nor the one who lacks understanding and recognition of it."

He, may Allaah preserve him, said,[49]

"We stand with complete surety and confidence, and all praise is due to Allaah, upon our way that we stand upon. Because we're upon the truth, upon the revealed book of our Lord, and the Sunnah of our Prophet, and the methodology of our righteous predecessors."

The sheikh, may Allaah preserve him, also said,[50]

"The believer who has certainty of the correctness of his religion, will not be affected by doubts about Islaam, as doubts about the religion only affect someone upon

---
[48] Definitive Responses to Doubts and Misconceptions that Have Arisen pg. 51
[49] The Obligation Of Adhering To That Body Of Muslims Upon The Truth. pg. 18
[50] The Correct Position of a Muslim Towards Trials, Societal demonstrations, and Political Revolutions: pg 11

hypocrisy or someone with very weak faith."

The failure to hold firmly to the original believers' way and the deficiencies this leads to within the Ummah as a whole have also been explained by the scholars. Sheikh al-Fauzaan explains in several of his lectures that from the clearly negative consequences of some Muslims turning away from the general methodology of the Messenger of Allaah as well as the implementation of that clear way by the first generations, is the appearance of division and splitting among the Muslim Ummah. He, may Allaah preserve him, said, [51]

"The original cause of division among the Muslims: Contradicting the methodology of the Salaf, the first three generations.

Firstly, contradicting the methodology of the Salaf from the Companions of the Messenger of Allaah, may Allaah's praise and salutations be upon him, and those who followed them. As the Salaf had a methodology which they preceded upon, a methodology in beliefs, a methodology in calling to Allaah, a methodology in enjoining the good and forbidding wrong-doing, and a methodology in legal judgment between the people. This general way and methodology is taken from the Book of Allaah and Sunnah of His Messenger, may Allaah's praise and salutations be upon him.

And this land, all praise is due to Allaah, has proceeded upon this methodology, and is well known far and wide, such that no one denies it except for the arrogant haughty individual. This land has proceeded upon this correct way and methodology, upon the methodology of the Salaf in its beliefs, in its efforts in calling to Allaah, the Most Glorified and the Most Exalted, in its enjoining the good and forbidding wrongdoing, and in

---
[51] Lectures in Aqeedah and Da'wah" page 406-407

its judging between the people according to what Allaah has revealed. All of this is a reality which is present and has not ceased in this land, all praise is due to Allaah, and no one denies this except the arrogant one.

'The Danger Of Imported Methodologies Which Oppose The Book And The Sunnah'

If we deny this minhaj, this methodology which the Salaf, the righteous first three generations were upon, and proceed to import and adopt various other methodologies from this outside country and from that foreign land, we will inevitably become divided. Such that every different group of people among us ends up having a separate methodology than the other groups of people also from among the Muslims, with each group declaring the others in error.

Why would this outcome be acceptable oh brothers? Are we not a single Ummah? Is not our religion only Islaam? Is not our methodology the way of the Messenger of Allaah, may Allaah's praise and salutations be upon him, and his Companions? Is not our guide and our source, and our reference the Book of Allaah and the Sunnah of the Messenger of Allaah, may Allaah's praise and salutations be upon him? If so then why do we import principles and concepts from this land and from that country?

In fact, it is rather obligatory that we export this sound methodology and path of Islaam which we stand upon to the other countries of the world. As Allaah, the Most High has said, ❖ **You [true believers in Islamic Monotheism, and real followers of Prophet Muhammad and his Sunnah] are the best of peoples ever raised up for mankind; you enjoin al-Ma'roof (Islaamic Monotheism and all that Islaam has ordained) and** *forbid al-Munkar (polytheism, disbelief and all that Islaam has forbidden), and you believe in Allaah.* ﴾-*(Surah Aal-'Imraan:110)*

He, may Allaah preserve him, also point out that,[52]

"We have no need to import and incorporate within our way and our methodology the practices of the disbelievers, nor any chaotic ways of those who disbelieve in Islaam."

In relation to this false idea of the need to reform and reshape Islaam in light of outside ideologies Sheikh Ibn Baadees, may Allaah have mercy upon him said, [53]

"The most perfect of nations is the one who beautifully understands how to preserve the good it already has, and also benefit from the good which other nations have in worldly matters."

The beliefs of Islaam, which distinguish the Muslim Ummah, are of central importance to our success as Muslims, yet many people neglect to properly learn them. Our correct beliefs formed the heart of the message of every single prophet, as they all called to the true and full worship of Allaah alone, specifically as He has commanded them, These evidenced beliefs call to the explicit required disbelief and rejection of any associates with Him.

Sheikh Saaleh Ibn Fauzaan, may Allaah preserve him, said,[54]

"It is required that we give attention to the affirmed practices of the Sunnah, and teaching beneficial knowledge and the correct beliefs of Islaam, teaching the beliefs held by the first three generations and everything that they stood upon."

Sheikh Rabee'a al-Madkhalee, may Allaah preserve him, emphasized what the leading scholars, as the true

---

[52] Definitive Responses to Doubts and Misconceptions that Have Arisen pg. 43
[53] Narrations of Benefit from Sheikh Ibn Baadees, vol.3 pg. 129
[54] Explanation of the Advice and Counsel of the Prophet: pg. 18

inheritors of the prophets, have always taught, in his own commentary of Usul as-Sunnah,

> *"The beliefs of Islaam which the various Messengers came with have a tremendous position in Islaam, indeed it is the very foundation of the religion of Islaam. It is the true criterion by which one distinguishes correct and valid worship from that which is incorrect and false.*
>
> *For this reason the scholars of Islaam, meaning the scholars of the people who adhered to the Sunnah and held firmly to the united body of Muslims upon the truth, have given priority and importance to clarifying what are these beliefs, explaining them, defending and protecting them, and calling to them. Likewise they have authored many works dedicated specifically to this subject, as well as incorporating many aspects of it throughout their general writings.*
>
> *...It is obligatory upon the students of knowledge to give priority to studying the correct beliefs, and the fundamentals which they are built upon....*
>
> *....From those summarized writing which were composed to explain these correct beliefs of Islaam is this present book which was written by Imaam Ahmad, may Allaah have mercy upon him, who is considered one of the leading scholars of the people of the Sunnah and Jamaa'ah of those Muslims who remained united upon the truth.....*
>
> *...So learn and know the high value of this Sunnah, and know and be aware of the value and status of the people of the Sunnah, holding fast to them, to their steadfast positions, and following in their footsteps. As, by Allaah, they stood upon the brilliant distinct path of guidance, following the Book of Allaah, and upon the Sunnah of*

the Messenger of Allaah, and upon the path of the Noble Companions and at the head whom were the Rightly Guided Khaleefahs.

...Hold firmly to this. Study this small book,... I ask that He benefit us through this book and as well as through others from the books of Islamic knowledge, and especially the books related to correct and authentic beliefs, the beliefs of the people of the Sunnah and adherence to the united body of Muslims upon the truth."

These correct fundamental beliefs are derived from revelation and from the essential prophetic understanding upon which each and every Muslim should inwardly build his life upon. Yet this does not means we neglect the many other important parts of Islaam, which the first Muslims understood, practiced, and embraced as their general way, or methodology of life upon submission to Allaah. The scholars have made clear that there is a single correct methodology which encompasses all the matters of Islaam which the Prophet himself stood upon. It not only includes select matters of guidance such as our beliefs, but also many other aspects of his guidance seen clearly throughout his entire life. What has occurred in our current century is that some groups and movements have abandoned significant parts of Islaam and replaced them with the views of their founders and group leaders. They want to join the core beliefs of Islaam with that specific newly devised methodology that they have come to stand upon. Sheikh Saaleh Ibn Fauzaan, may Allaah preserve him, was asked, **"It is correct to say that it is possible to combine between having the beliefs held by the first three generations of Islaam, the Salaf, and adopting a modern day methodology such as from the group the Muslim Brotherhood, or the group Jamaa'at at-Tableegh?"** Sheikh Saaleh Ibn Fauzaan, replied, [55]

"It can never be possible to join between two fundamentally

[55] Definitive Responses to Doubts and Misconceptions that Have Arisen: pg. 42

opposing and conflict ways, absolutely not."

Sheikh Rabee'a al-Madkhaalee, may Allaah preserve him, was also asked about this specific misunderstanding, **"Is the way or methodology of the first generations restricted to only issues of belief, or does it also encompass the entire religion and whatever that contains of the Sharee'ah way of rectification?"** He replied, [56]

"The way or methodology of the first generations encompasses beliefs and actual ways, or as may be said our belief and our way or methodology which the Prophet Muhammad came with, may Allaah's praise and salutations be upon him. This includes beliefs, acts of ritual worship, regular dealing, matters of governing and economics, and all the paths of life which possess this true way which is proceeded upon in seeking to rectifying our affairs. It is not permissible to take out from this general path or remove from it any aspect or any realm or area or intentionally leave applying its guidance from any situation of the different situations of life.

Therefore the statement made by some of those who have innovated in the religion and people of various modern groups, [I am following the Salaf in my beliefs but I am Ikhwaanee (following the false principles of the Muslims Brotherhood organization) in my organizational methodology and way.] only deceives the individual himself and deceives the worshipers of Allaah in general.

As the Messenger of Allaah, may Allaah praise and salutations be upon him, only had a single set of beliefs, along with a single way and methodology. For this reason, it is not permissible for a Muslim to turn and go away from either one of these two aspects. And if he leaves both them or even one of them, then he in fact leaves from the way of the Salaf, the early generations,

---

[56] From a telephone lecture dated 02-25-1416

whether he wants and intend to leave it or does not intend to and denies that he has left it."

Understanding and adhering to the general methodology of the Sunnah as well as its beliefs guides a striving Muslim to turn away from the misconceptions related to Islaam and its people like the false beliefs mentioned earlier. Understanding its characteristics and hallmarks enables a Muslim to recognize the half understandings and distorted priorities of any of the many misguided speakers, self-satisfied writers, politically oriented Muslim groups, and innovated movements that are present in our age, as well as those more sophisticated offshoots likely to emerge in the future. The Muslim who comes to understand that Islaam has a established knowledge based methodology, not simply inward beliefs and limited rituals to be implemented however one arbitrarily chooses, is faced with the choice to accept everything which the beauty of Islaam offers, as done by the first generations of believers, or to turn away from some aspects of it and follow their various ideas, concepts, and desires whether personal or coming from someone else. Those who knowingly turn away from one aspect of the clear methodology of the Prophet, do so at the increasing dangerous price of eventually turning away from more and more aspects of the guidance of the revealed religion of Islaam.

This is what has happened historically to many sects that emerged a continual increase and expansion of their misguidance. Among such sects, there is no doubt that the sect of the Shee'ah, had corrupt beliefs that lead to the development of their corrupt methodology generally, eventually leading them to attack the Companions as a whole specifically, may Allaah be pleased with all of the Companions. In doing so this sect are, in fact, attacking Islaam through attacking those who carried it, those righteous first Muslims who understood, practiced, and transmitted Islaam to humanity and to the rest of the future Muslim Ummah. By attacking the very connection we have to the Qur'aan and the clarifying Sunnah, they directly undermine the original beliefs and methodology which our beloved Prophet, may the praise and salutations of Allaah be upon him, lived and then died upon.

The clarification of our beliefs and general way by Imaam Ahmad, and the many scholars in our time who have commentaries upon his treatise, is undoubtedly an incredible jihad defending Islaam and the established boundaries and borders of its correct beliefs and proper methodology. Sheikh 'Abdur-Rahman Ibn Sa'dee, one of the well known teachers of Sheikh al-'Utheimeen, may Allaah have mercy upon him, similarly said,[57]

> *"There are two types of Jihaad, that Jihaad by which you intend to bring about the general rectification of the Muslims and to correct their shortcomings and errors within their beliefs, their characters, their manners, and all the different affairs of their religious and worldly life, through educating and cultivating them upon beneficial knowledge.*
>
> *This form is from the foundations of all other forms of Jihaad and its main pillar, it is what the second category of Jihaad is built upon, which is that physical Jihaad intended to defend Islaam and the Muslims against aggressors towards them, coming from the disbelievers, the hypocrites, the disbelieving apostates and all of the enemies of the religion who choose to fight against the Muslims. As such these two types of Jihaad, Jihaad with the proofs and evidences using one's tongue, and the second type of Jihaad using whatever military weapons for defense which are suitable and sufficient according to the time and period it needs to be undertaken."*

---

[57] From the Obligation of Establish Cooperation Among the Muslims, pg. 5

Methodology is of fundamental importance in following the Sunnah

It is important to try and bring forward concrete examples that show the reality of conflicting methodologies among those who attribute themselves to Islaam. This is in order to show that fundamental differences in one's methodology of Islaam always lead to only harm, because they reflect distance from the original guidance of Islaam. Such practical examples can show us the importance of adhering to that specific methodology which agrees in detail with what the Prophet and his Companions stood upon, because their guided way and methodology is what enabled them to spread the liberating guidance of Islaam to the entire world.

From the examples of these essential differences is an evidenced discussion of some of the differences between the sects of the Shee'ah and the Sunnees in their understanding and practice of Islaam. This is especially true in consideration of the recent historical efforts to minimize the documented differences between the Sunnees and the Shee'ah, and a push towards having Muslims simply attribute themselves to a general Islaam which none can disagree with. Many today wrongly echo the empty claim that there are only minor differences between the people of the Sunnah and those upon the innovated religion of the Shee'ah. They openly claim that these 'minor' differences should not actually prevent our unity and cooperation.

This exact sentiment reflects aspects of the general methodology proceeded upon and promoted by one of the groups of misguidance present today, the Muslim Brotherhood organization. As was acknowledged by the 'Umar at-Talmisaanee, the third general leader of the Muslim Brotherhood organization, that one of the original focuses and objectives of Hasan al-Banna was to unite between the Sunnees and the Shee'ah.[58] Sheikh Hammaad Ibn Muhammad al-Ansaaree, may Allaah have mercy upon him, speaking about the practical results and consequences of this said,[59]

> *"I had previously come to hear some time ago that the Muslim Brotherhood organization had in the time of the King Farouk come to stand upon the understanding, as well as bringing forward of the claim, that the Raafidhah should be counted as one of the legitimate schools from the schools of thought among the Muslims, and that it be incorporated within and held as part of this Ummah.*
>
> *It is for this reason that they, this organization, were those who assisted the revolution initiated by Khomaynee, and were tremendously pleased by it. They would say, [There is no Islaam other than that Islaam put forward by him.]"*

Due to this organization's founder lacking a firm grounding in evidenced authentic Sharee'ah knowledge from its guiding scholars both past and in his age, he falsely held that the differences between these two sects were not connected to the foundation of essential Islamic beliefs! He wrongly believed that the distinctions were only in lesser secondary matters, as such it was allegedly possible for reconciliation and true unity to be achieved between these two sects.

---

[58] This was mentioned in his book 'Dhakiyaat Laa Mudhakaraat pg. 249-250'. However, this legacy of falsehood was in recent years again acknowledged and the cooperation between the Muslim Brotherhood organization and the Shee'ah again reaffirmed in what is seen of the publication of the 'Amaan Papers', which stressed the inclusion of every sect of the Shee'ah among Muslim Ummah, and wrongly legitimized their beliefs and jurisprudence. Among its signatories, supporting its content, was both the supreme spiritual leaders of Iran Khamaynee (the successor to Khomaynee), many Iranian Shee'ah clerics, as well as the current head of the Muslim Brotherhood in Jordan.

[59] Al-Majmu'a from the Biography of Sheikh Hammaad Ibn Muhammad al-Ansaaree: Number 111

Yet, the overwhelming mountain of facts and proofs, which dispute this dangerous claim, have been documented by the scholars of the Sunnah in this and previous centuries. Sheikh Ibn Baaz, may Allaah have mercy upon him, was asked, [60] ***"Esteemed sheikh in light of your knowledge of the accounts of the Raafidhah sect throughout history, what is your position towards the belief and idea that there should be rapprochement between the people of the Sunnah and the Raafidhah?"*** He replied,

> *"A coming together between the Raafidhah and the people of the Sunnah is not at all possible. Because their fundamental beliefs oppose each other. The essential beliefs of the people of the Sunnah and adherence to the Jamaa'ah is establishing the worship of Allaah, and having purity of intention in our worship such that it is done solely for Him alone, the Most Perfect and the Most High. Their belief, the people of the Sunnah, is that it is impermissible to supplicate to anyone alongside of Allaah, not to one of the angels close to Him, nor to one of the dead prophets whom He sent. They also hold that it is only Allaah, the Most Perfect and the Most High, who possesses true knowledge of the hidden unseen world.*
>
> *From the essential beliefs of the people of the Sunnah and adherence to the Jamaa'ah is having a strong love for the Companions, of the Prophet, may Allaah be pleased with them all, and being pleased with them. It is having full faith that generally they are the best of the creation of Allaah, below the level of Allaah's prophets. It is believing that specifically the best among them was Abu Bakr as-Siddeeq, then 'Umar, then 'Uthmaan, and then 'Alee, may Allaah be pleased with them all.*
>
> *The Raafidhah oppose all of this, so it is not possible*

---

[60] Collection of Rulings and Various Statements of Sheikh Ibn Baaz, vol. 5

> *or conceivable to join between the two. Just as it is not possible to join between the Jews, the Christians, the Pagans, along with the people of the Sunnah; it is also impossible to truly join together the Raafidhah and the people of the Sunnah. This is due to those conflicting essential beliefs in central issues of Islaam which we have just mentioned and indicated."*

This is also born witness to in the documented modern history by the negligence of their modern leaders toward even properly giving priority to the fundamental five pillars of Islaam. As Sheikh Muhammad Baazmool explained about them, [61]

> *"Did you know that Khomaynee, the one who inspired the Iranian revolution, up until the very day he died, never made the obligatory Hajj? Did you also know that Khamaynee, the leader who succeeded Khomaynee in Iran after his death, up until this very day has still never made the obligatory pilgrimage?"*

We need to consider one of the roots of the problem of why there are so many points of conflict and disagreement, which is actually their opposition to the correct beliefs of Islaam. To do so we can refer to those scholars such as Sheikh Ehsan Alahee Dhaaher, may Allaah have mercy upon him, who specialized in producing scholastic evidenced discourses in defence of the Sunnah. He, may Allaah have mercy upon him, scholastically excelled in documenting these claimed insignificant differences, so meticulously from the original sources of the Shee'ah themselves. The Shee'ah who could not respond with any authentic knowledge based rebuttals or Sharee'ah proofs, eventually resorted to assassinating him in order to silence his continual repeated evidenced powerful exposures of their historical and modern falsehoods and deceptions. The reality is as the esteemed Sheikh Zayd al-Madkhalee,

---
[61] 'Did you know? #89' from the sheik's website

may Allaah, the Most High, have mercy on him, has mentioned, [62]

> *"In every age and period there are means by which by good and evil is spread and propagated. In past ages the means of this were generally through circulating books, giving sermons, having circles of learning, and what is similar to this. As for our current age, then the means and methods for spreading knowledge have certainly become varied and diverse.*
>
> *One finds today that the people of the Sunnah spread beneficial knowledge which produces righteous deeds, they exemplify this in their understanding of the truth generally and in its essential details, in implementing and circulating it, inviting to it, and being patient with the difficulties encountered while doing so. This applies to all the means that they have at their disposal.*
>
> *One finds that the people of falsehood likewise spread their falsehood whether this is from forbidden acts of shirk, innovated new beliefs and practices into Islaam, or matters that are generally corrupt in its varied forms. They bring forth and spread corruptions in the area of essential beliefs of the Muslim, corruptions in how righteous deeds should be carried out, and other different forms of corruption that fight openly against the Sunnah and its people, without showing any fear of Allaah, nor any shyness from Him, exalted is He in His transcendence above creation."*

To illustrate an example of this and show the importance of correct evidenced essential beliefs, and how they reflect of the importance of the methodology of Islaam; let us look at some statements from a scholar of misguidance who is undoubtedly considered the most famous Shee'ah scholar of modern times - Khomaynee, may Allaah give him what

---
[62] al-Aweebah al-Athereeyah, pg. 20

he deserves. Khomaynee was someone well known for promoting this false call to a general attribution to Islaam which purposely ignores true significant differences between sects and negates any need for a clear foundation of actual shared beliefs and practices. He said,[63]

[*We are one with Sunnee Muslims as we're all Muslims and brothers. If one speaks of dividing word between us as Muslims you must know he is either insane or hopes to cause conflicts between Muslims. There is not a case as Shee'ah and separate Sunnee at all - since we are all brothers." (Sahifa Imaam v.6 p.133)*]

This call, the deceptive call for unquestioning "brotherhood" between the Sunnees and the Shee'ah, is based and founded upon his outward claim that, in beliefs or other matters, there are no insurmountable divisions or differences between the Sunnees and the Shee'ah, only minor differences or historical disagreements. Yet nothing could be further from the truth. This belief is itself, firstly, inaccurate historically, when examining the beliefs and principles of Islaam held by each sect, throughout the centuries. Secondly, as scholastically demonstrated, there are many widely differing practices and principles of Islaam between the two sects as shown by their scholars' words and writings. It is a ever widening gulf that started in the first century of Islaam as the Shee'ah first separated from the Jamaa'ah, but also continually widened by them over the centuries.

Additionally, this statement of Khomaynee is a clear example of a type of subtle deception that our guiding upright scholars upon the Sunnah have warned us about, in order that we not fall into mistaking every call raised with the title of "Islaam!" as truly reflecting our beloved religion. Rather they have stressed to us the importance of learning the core beliefs of Islaam which the Companions

---

[63] As quotes on the official Iranian government page for Khomaynee –English Language version

held and then transmitted to the next generation of Muslims, and so on in every period of our history- based firmly upon the Qur'aan and authentic Sunnah. For this reason, with a discerning eye let us take a moment to ask and investigate. Is it true that there aren't any significant beliefs dividing the Sunnees from the Shee'ah? Are there actually any examples of truly differing fundamental practices? Is the current disunity really only based upon only based on old historical quarrels of little importance in the modern world?

Alhamdulillah, as mentioned, the scholars upon the Sunnah have produced many detailed books outlining the concrete differences between the Shee'ah- and the many deviant sects and groups connected to them- and the people of the Sunnah, who remained upon the original general beliefs and methodology held by the Companions, may Allaah be pleased with them all. The following section shows that without question there are concrete differences between the correct beliefs of the people of the Sunnah, based upon revelation sent down from Allaah, and the intricate web of corrupt innovated beliefs held and propagated by the sect of the Shee'ah. They are in reality as different as night is from day, despite the twisted justifications offered for their new beliefs and practices.

Take a moment to consider the following specific beliefs, which shed light on this claim that there was no true differences between Sunnees and Shee'ah, which Khomaynee outwardly proclaimed. The first verified quote of his is a statement which directly opposes the fundamental message of Islaam, taught by each and every one of the sent prophets and messengers. Khomaynee, in his one of his most influential books 'al-Hukoomatul-lslamiyyah (the Islamic Government)', claimed that the Twelve Imaams of the Shee'ah have been given by Allaah a level above all the angels and all the prophets that Allaah ever sent to humanity, so much so that these twelve

Shee'ah "Imaams" control the very individual atoms of the universe. He stated what means, [64]

[*Certainly, the Imaam commands a noble station and lofty position; a creative vicegerency to whose rule and power submit the very atoms of all creation. And an essential tenet of our Shi'ite sect is that the Imaams have a position which is reached neither by the angels [in the highest heaven] nor by any commissioned messenger of Allaah.*]

This clearly opposes the belief held by Ahlus-Sunnah that although the prophets and messengers are the best of Allaah's creation and the highest level of human excellence, and had miracles by Allaah's permission, none of the creation share in the power of Allaah over His creation even to the smallest degree. Indeed this is an astounding claim, that Allaah gave these twelve imaams, one of whom the Shee'ah believe remains alive in a hidden state, personal powers over the very atoms of creation. This is a claim which no prophet or messenger made throughout human history!

Every sincere Muslim should ask themselves whether this is found in the teaching of their beloved Prophet. He should also ask himself whether Alee, may Allaah be pleased with him, ever claimed this power, and if he possessed it why did he not use it for Islaam? Generally there are several statements of their Shee'ah scholars asserting that these twelve Imaams were higher in merit than all the prophets and messengers Allaah sent to humanity expect for the Prophet Muhammad. However, in a twisted circle of falsehood, their claimed reason for this exception is that he was not only a prophet and messenger, but had been blessed to join along with the other twelve in being an "Imaam" also!

In a related statement that negates the completion and perfection of Islaam, Khomaynee also falsely called the Muslim Ummah to follow the individual commands from

---
[64] Khomaynee, al-Hukoomat ul-Islamiyyah, pp. 52-53

these twelve Shee'ah imaams, whom they falsely believe to be infallible and free from committing any errors or mistakes. He calls the Muslims to follow their commands just as if they were following the revelation sent down by Allaah. Khomaynee stated, [65]

[The teachings and directives of the (twelve) Imaams are just like those of the Qur'aan; it is compulsory on one to follow them and carry them out.]

This fundamental absolute contradiction to what the people who love and adhere to the Sunnah believe is another significant indicates that the two sects actually differ in their fundamental methodology of Islaam. The people of the Sunnah hold that no one is followed absolutely other than The Messenger of Allaah, Muhammad, because no one else was made infallible in their statements and actions. Both of these serious issues, which are only two of many, are stark reminders of the serious and urgent need for the Muslims to study the correct beliefs from the original sources of Islaam, and understand what opposes those correct beliefs from falsehood, in order to proceed upon the correct general methodology of Islaam in their lives.

Lastly, we consider a third example which also shows that there is little substance behind this claimed desire for unity between the two sects. It is an example which exposes their ugly hatred for the best of the Prophet's Companions, whom we, the people of the Sunnah, love dearly. When speaking to youth, in his own nation, upon his own corrupt methodology Khomaynee mentioned that if the Shee'ah were able to gain control over the sacred cities in the lands of Islaam, he had specific plans for graves of two best Companions, whom we know are from the most honored of people in creation after the prophets and messengers,[66]

---

[65] Khomaynee, al-Hukoomat ul-Islamiyyah, pp. 52-53

[66] Source : From an address given by Khomaynee to a youth rally a cited in the work 'Khomaynees and Islaam', page 8 by Abu Rehan Ziaur Rahman Farooqi

[... *when as a conqueror I will enter Makkah and Madeenah, the first thing to be done at that time by me would be to dig out two idols (Abu Bakr and 'Umar) lying by the side of the Prophet's grave.*]

It should be pointed out that, through the scholar's refutations of his various statements, it is clear that Khomaynee's public writings also contain several additional attacks against both Abu Bakr and 'Umar, may Allaah be pleased with them both.[67] Indeed, some of their scholars teach a supplication to the general Shee'ah that curses these two righteous worshippers of Allaah and pillars of the first community of Islaam. These false claims and attacks against the two of them form the foundation for his hatred found in his wicked statement mentioned, meaning calling them idols to be dug up and expelled from their current honorable graves where the Mother of the Believers 'Aishah, may Allaah be pleased with all of them, allowed them to be buried near the Messenger, may the praise and salutations of Allaah be upon him.

The honest and discerning Muslim is obliged by the evidence, to admit that it is not only in a minor difference in a few fiqh or jurisprudence rulings, but clearly opposing positions about the very sources of the Sharee'ah, the nature of leadership Allaah placed within Islaam, what each sect holds to be the unchanging beliefs and references for Islaam, and many other core issues. It should be apparent that any knowledgeable Sunnee scholar quoting the Qur'aan and Sunnah- from the well know books of hadeeth, and any Shee'ah scholar quoting from their books and giving precedence the statements of their alleged infallible twelve Shee'ah Imaams will undoubtedly conflict with each other in most aspects of what they consider and call to as Islaam both inwardly and outwardly. As a smokescreen, sometimes those Muslims

---

[67] For further information about his various slanders against the Companions, may Allaah be pleased with them all, refer to the various refutations of Khomaynee which the scholars of the Sunnah have authored.

who reject the extremism of the Shee'ah towards the restricted single line of descendants of 'Alee the Shee'ah have attached themselves to, are wrongly labeled by the Shee'ah, as 'Naasabees'. Yet Sheikh Muqbil ibn Haadee al-Waadi'ee, may Allaah have mercy upon him, made clear the correct definition and understanding of this term,[68]

> *"The questioner is asking about the meaning of the term 'Naasabee'. We say, this term means: that individual who is characterized by enmity and hatred for the descendants of members of the household of the prophet Muhammad, may Allaah's praise and salutation be upon him and his family, and who are characterized by fighting against them, whether this be through their hands and actions, or through speaking against them with their tongues and speech. This is the meaning of the term Naasabee.*
>
> *Moreover the scholars of hadeeth and the people upon the Sunnah have continually opposed and fought against those who were Naasabee and therefore considered innovators in the religion, just as they have opposed and fought against those who were Shee'ah and considered innovators in the religion."*

To consider this third point of misguidance in more detail, one can easily compare the difference between the position of Abu Bakr and 'Umar in the eyes of Khomaynee as stated above, and the position of Abu Bakr and 'Umar in the eyes of the Messenger of Allaah, may the praise and salutations be upon him and his household; as part of testing and examining the claim that the beliefs of the Shee'ah are not really that different than those who adhere to the Sunnah. The Salaf in general gave tremendous importance to rejecting the false claims against the Companions which are commonly echoed by the Shee'ah and those affected by their unevidenced distortions of

---
[68] Tuhfat al-Mujeeb 'alaa Asi'lah al-Haadhir wal-Ghareeb, pg. 25

Islaam. As Muhammad al-Firyabee, may Allaah have mercy upon him, mentioned,[69]

> "I heard Sufyan say: If anyone thinks that 'Alee, may Allaah be pleased with him, was more deserving for the Caliphate than both of them, he attributed error to Abu Bakr, 'Umar, the Muhajirun (Immigrants), and the Ansar (Helpers) Allaah be pleased with all of them. Such that I think that with this belief none of his actions will rise to Heaven."

For a more detailed examination of this dangerous falsehood, please refer to the last appendix for a number of authentic narrations about the position and merit of Abu Bakr and 'Umar, may Allaah be pleased with them all, whose meaning is clear for any sincere Muslim.

This issue of the place, knowledge, and general excellence of the Companions is not only important to mention, but essential and central to the correct methodology of Islaam. Additionally, this subject is directly related to the initial statement of Imaam Ahmad in the beginning of Usul as-Sunnah, where he defines the fundamentals of Sunnah and correct Islaam to generally be that which the Companions understood and practiced, may Allaah be pleased with all of them. These selected authentic narrations about Abu Bakr and 'Umar, may Allaaah be pleased with them both, found in authentic sources acknowledged by this Ummah, continue to guide the Muslims who turned to them to see exactly whom our Messenger counseled us to follow, and whom he commanded us to take as our examples as Muslims striving upon the truth.

For this reason, when weighing and considering the earlier statement of Khomaynee and the many statements of our Messenger mentioned in the appendix, the question before every sincere Muslim is, whose position towards these two are we to accept? Do we accept the position

---

[69] Sunan Abu Dawud:4630

of Messenger of Allaah, as shown in the many authentic hadeeth mentioned, from our Prophet who was guided and directed by Allaah, our Lord Who knows what is in the hearts of all men, in everything he, the Prophet, said? Or do we accept the position of a misguided shaytaan from among the leaders of falsehood and misguidance in this century, may Allaah give him what he deserved, Khomaynee? Indeed, for the one whom Allaah grants guidance, the question truly needs no answer.

Khomaynee, in his subtle treachery towards Islaam, said about Abu Bakr and 'Umar that they opposed the guidance of Islaam and the dictates of the Qur'aan, while the many statements of our Prophet say that they both reflected the highest levels the guidance of Islaam, exemplified the Qur'aan truly and steadfastly, and that Allaah blessed them to be central to the success of Islaam. There is little doubt that this form of misguidance mentioned generally by Ibn Taymeeyah, may Allaah have mercy upon him, in one of his works considered a hallmark refutation of the Shee'ah, applies here to Khomaynee,[70]

> *"The one who turns away and strays from the light of the guidance of the Sunnah which Allaah sent down to His messenger, undoubtedly he inevitably keeps falling into the murky well of darkness that is innovations in the religion, with one misguiding innovation being fabricated and arranged on top of another."*

Furthermore, fully pulling the cover off the hollow claim that the Shee'ah, like the people of the Sunnah, sincerely follow and love the Messenger of Allaah, Sheikh Muhammad Baazmool said,[71]

> *"Do the Raafidhah, those who believe in twelve infallible imaams, who are present in Iran today love the Messenger of Allaah, may Allaah's praise and salutations*

---

[70] Minhaj as-Sunnah: vol. 6, pg. 315
[71] From the Facebook page of Sheikh Muhammad Ibn 'Umar Baazmool 11-28-17

be upon him?

If they truly loved the Messenger of Allaah, may Allaah's praise and salutations be upon him, they would not curse and slander the Mother of the believers 'A'ishah, may Allaah be pleased with her, and falsely accuse her of adultery!

If they truly loved him, they would not curse and speak against his Companions, may Allaah be pleased with them all, the most significant of which are Abu Bakr and 'Umar, may Allaah be pleased with them both.

If they truly loved him, they would never nationally celebrate the disbelieving holiday of their ancestors, the Persian Magians, and turn away from being satisfied with the two affirmed holidays of the first Muslims.

If they truly loved him, they would not destroy those masjids calling to the Sunnah within the country of Iran. Nor would they prohibit the Sunnee Muslims from performing Salaat al-Jumu'ah within the capital of their country Tehran. These people have no relationship or connection to Islaam, may Allaah fight against them because of their deceptions and numerous pretenses!"

The Companions of the last prophet and messenger form the basis of the Jamaa'ah of Muslims we have been ordered to adhere to, and anyone who openly attacks those righteous Muslims who first fought for, struggled for, and lived for Islaam, attacks Islaam at its roots. This honorable position of the Companions is a central tenet and aspect of the belief of those who adhere to the Sunnah. As Imaam Ahmad, may Allaah have mercy upon him, himself mentions within the text of Usul as-Sunnah,

51.[72] *And whoever disparages and belittles even a single*

---

[72] The division and numbering used for the text of Usul as-Sunnah is specific to this course book and is not found in the original Arabic text.

one of the Companions of the Messenger of Allaah, may Allaah's praise and salutations be upon him, or dislikes a Companion on account of something that he did, or mentions his shortcomings, then he is an innovator in the religion. Until he changes to become someone who asks for Allaah's mercy upon all of them, and until his heart is free from any ill-will, and supportive and truly inclined towards them.

Imaam Ahmad, may Allaah have mercy upon him, as a leading scholar affirmed the position standing, and role of the Companions, may Allaah be pleased with them all, as essential to the correct methodology of Islaam. In comparison the position of Khomaynee upon misguidance is clear, as is the position of all those who oppose the Companions, and the Islaam they called to, whether individuals, movements, groups, or sects, whether past, present, or in the future. They are callers to misguidance who are astray and leading others astray.

Furthermore, Khomaynee's statements, are a very clear example of proceeding upon a corrupt methodology within your understanding and therefore your practice of Islaam. His understanding is something that would never lead to the unity of the Muslims nor their true success, but only pushes us further down to road towards continued humiliation and ruin. Every sincere Muslim should come to realize that the removal of disunity and hope for unity which every sincere Muslim wants cannot not achieved through eloquent empty calls to adhere to a 'general' Islaam as Khomaynee publicly did. The scholars have shown us that such a general wide understanding of Islaam, with many different interpretations and several varying distorted practical applications among the Muslims, cannot lead to actual unity between the Sunnees and the Shee'ah, nor generally to unity within the Muslim Ummah as a whole.

In should be noted that here in western countries there are those who acknowledge the differences between the modern day Shee'ah and the Sunnees, but believe we should not discuss them at all. They believe that even if some people who consider themselves Muslim declare the majority of the Companions of the beloved Prophet, may the praise and salutations of Allaah, to be those apostated from Islaam, it still should not be discussed. An example of a caller to this corrupt thinking and destructive methodology is the American Muslim Hamza Yusuf who said,[73]

[You know the Shee'ah, I consider them they're our brothers in the religion. Its an old debate and I'm not going to resolve it if the greatest scholars in the history of Islaam couldn't resolve it, we are not going to resolve it. We shouldn't be under that illusion. And we should just have peaceful coexistence. You know they have their mosques, and if they come to our mosques, marhaban (welcome). They are welcome to pray with us and we shouldn't get into fights or arguments with them.

We certainly should not discuss the issues that create the animosity, about the Sahaabah, or 'Aishah, radhi Allahu anha, or any of those things. And if you don't ask, you know you won't have a problem, if you start asking you have problems...]

This corrupt belief, born from other false beliefs, is that cooperation not clarification should be our goal despite these serious differences regarding the fundamentals of this blessed religion. Consider, oh sincere reader, a practical example of his false call, that being an attempt at cooperation of "united" Sunnees and Shee'ah in a single masjid. What would they teach in their classes generally? What would they call the young Muslims to study specifically? Would they teach the beliefs found by referring back to the Qur'aan and Sunnah, or those found

---

[73] As found in a his voice on the internet and affirmed by his other statements

when referring back to the Shee'ah books of teachings attributed to the twelve alleged infallible "Imaams"? As the Shee'ah fundamentally differ from the people adhering to the original Sunnah in this. Should we not discuss the sources of Islaam and the place of the treasures chests of pure Sunnah like Saheeh al-Bukhaaree? Or should it be avoided?

This question also extends to the practices of Islaam. How would this "general" Islaam be practiced? What would they teach and practice about praying to Allaah through the intercession of the righteous and visiting the raised tombs of the dead Muslims to ask them supplicate and intercede? As again, the Shee'ah fundamentally differ from the people adhering to the original Sunnah in this.

How would they pray together in the five obligatory ritual prayers, and teach others, including new Muslims, to perform these obligatory prayer? Would they teach a new Muslim that they should perform his obligatory prayer by always prostrating upon a clay tablet often called a 'turbah' which is often made from the clay taken of the land in Karbala, a clay tablet that sometimes has upon it "Ya Fatimah az-Zahrah"? Do we tell them that this is the Islaam that Allaah sent His Messenger to bring to humanity?[74] Would we teach new Muslims that this is a "good innovation" which improves Islaam, even though there was not a single Muslim Companion including 'Alee, may Allaah be pleased with him, who prayed with such a 'turbah'? As again, the Shee'ah fundamentally differ from the people adhering to the original Sunnah in these claims and practices. Should we not discuss how to implement and practice this pillar of Islaam, this essential worship which will be the first thing judged on the Day of Reckoning?

What would they, the administration of such a masjid, hold

---

[74] In fact it is affirmed that there are distinct "Prayer Kits" for Shee'ah for sale on the internet that include a "turbah" for prostration.

was valid and correct in matters or marriage and divorce, including the validity of temporary marriage for the people attending that masjid? Would such a masjid permit temporary marriages that simply expire after a certain amount of time, whether that be a day, a week, perhaps a month or a year? As again, the Shee'ah fundamentally differ from the people adhering to the original Sunnah in this. Should we not discuss whether or not short term temporary marriages are from the enduring guidance of Islaam? Without question, in terms of numerous beliefs and practices, the methodology of the religion of the Shee'ah has no consistent principled or practical reference and model within the evidenced methodology of the Prophet of Islaam, Muhammad, may Allaah's praise and salutations be upon him and his household.

These few examples show the impossibility of sincere practical cooperation even in a single masjid of those who truly hold Shee'ah beliefs with those who have- with those who have and strive to practice authentic knowledge of Islaam. Consider those misguided Muslims who say, [Don't speak of these matters!] and chose to ignore the many serious significant false beliefs of the misguided sect of the Shee'ah. Either they approve and permit such teachings and practices similar to the above mentioned, which is a naturally bitter fruit of the cooperation between the Sunnees and Shee'ah as "brothers" or they do not approve but chose to conceal them, or are ignorant of these serious issues altogether. As the scholars mentioned earlier, true unity, whether in principle or practice, will only be achieved through adhering to the original methodology of Islaam the first Muslims were upon, that original path and way upon which Allaah granted success to the Companions, while the Prophet stood over them guiding their hearts, tongues, hands, steps, and direction. They were those whom Allaah supported, gave victory to, and praised in the Qur'aan. There are the first Jamaa'ah we have been command to hold firmly to within the authentic words of our beloved Messenger.

It is essential to take careful note that this separation does not only apply to the Shee'ah. Rather the importance of considering both their beliefs and their methodology, applies to every group, movement, or sect that stands upon something different that what the noble Companions stood upon. As previously mentioned, the words and deeds of our Prophet are unmistakable in calling us to acknowledge that there are distinguishing characteristics of those who stand upon the unchanging truth and proceed with the people of truth, from those who separated from them. The validity of these distinguishing characteristics have a clear basis and foundation not only in the authentic narrations of the Messenger of Allaah, but how they were understood, explained, and practised by the leading Companions. In Saheeh Muslim it is narrated,[75]

> *"On the authority of Yahya b. Ya'mur that the first man who discussed qadr (divine decree) in Basra was Ma'bad al-Juhani. I along with Humaid b. 'Abdur-Rahman Himyaree had set out for pilgrimage or for 'Umrah and so said to ourselves:*
>
> *Should it so happen that we come into contact with one of the Companions of the Messenger of Allaah, we shall ask him about what is talked by people concerning divine decree. Accidentally we came across 'Abdullah ibn 'Umar ibn al-Khattab while he was entering the mosque. My companion and I surrounded him. One of us stood on his right and the other stood on his left. I expected that my companion would allow me to speak. So I said:*
>
> *Abu 'Abdur-Rahman! There have appeared some people in our land who recite the Qur'aan and pursue knowledge. And then described about their affairs,*

---

[75] Saheeh Muslim: no.8

afterwards I added: They (such people) claim that there is no such thing as divine decree and events are not predestined. ..."

Here we stop a moment to quickly consider the response today by a sincere Muslim who wrongly, lacking authentic knowledge, does not consider details of such differences in beliefs nor the methodologies they come from important. How many of them would say [What is truly important is that we are all Muslims.] or claim that [What is essential brother, is not smaller issues, but that we united in the face of our enemies.]

Yet consider carefully the response of the eminent Companion, 'Abdullah son of an eminent Companion 'Umar, both from among the early scholars of Islaam, may Allaah be pleased with them both. He, 'Abdullah ibn 'Umar, offered the following in response to their explanation and inquiry about those sincere misguided people,

> *"...'When you happen to meet such people tell them that I have nothing to do with them and they have nothing to do with me. And verily they are in no way responsible for my belief.'*
>
> *'Abdullah ibn 'Umar then swore by Him (the Lord) saying: 'If any one of them (who does not believe in the divine decree) had with him gold equal to the bulk of the mountain of Uhud and spent it in the way of Allaah, Allaah would not accept it unless he affirmed his faith in divine decree...' "*

This is the distinction of the original revealed truth and those who remained upon it, found in the words of this noble Companion, may Allaah be abundantly pleased with him. This is what has been explained in detail in the writings of the leading scholars of the different centuries upon the correct methodology of Islaam, and what is intended within this course book based upon the text Usul as-Sunnah. The clear explanations of the leading scholars upon the Sunnah, reject and refute the claim of those who call to a general Muslim unity between anyone and everyone who merely verbally attributes himself to Islaam to even the smallest degree. Indeed, as shown above, those who were involved with gaining knowledge of Islaam but rejected some of its core affirmed beliefs, were not accepted nor approved of by the Companions. As shown by 'Abdullah ibn 'Umar saying,

> *"...When you happen to meet such people tell them that I have nothing to do with them and they have nothing to do with me. And verily they are in no way responsible for my belief."*

Rather, true unity can only be based upon clarity of shared authentic fundamental beliefs including the affirmation of Allaah's decree, and conformance to the general methodology of the 'believers way' which has been followed by a successful group of Muslims in every generation. Sufyaan Ibn 'Uyainah, may Allaah have mercy upon him, said,[76]

> *"As for the Messenger of Allaah, may Allaah praise and salutations be upon him, his guidance is the greater scale, upon which things are placed in front of and compared to. All matters must be weighed against his character, his life history, and his guidelines. Whatever agrees with that then it is considered to be from what is correct and from truth, and whatever differs with that is considered incorrect and from falsehood."*

The modern scholastic explanations of the early texts written by the scholars of the Salaf, explain these essential matters about Islaam, and are strong fortresses that can protect a Muslim from being assaulted by the many doubts

---
[76] al-Jaama' al-Akhlaaq ar-Raawee wa Aadaab as-Saamee'a by Khateeb al-Baghdadee: vol. 1 pg. 79

and common misconceptions that Shaytaan and his party beautify, call to and spread among Muslims today.

THERE IS A SINGLE STRAIGHT PATH AND MANY PATHS STRAYING TO THE RIGHT AND LEFT OF IT

As is seen in the words of the scholars, and often reflected in our day to day lives as Muslims, one of the common causes that often prevents many Muslims from gaining steadfastness within Islaam is a deficiency in our understanding and level of evidenced knowledge of our religion. By this meaning many Muslims do not have firm knowledge about important aspects of the transmitted path of guidance that they want and struggle to proceed upon. It is a common disease today, which many people have been afflicted with, of wrongly believing that their own patchwork "personal understanding" of Islaam is enough and sufficient for them. This is regardless of what has been added or taken away from their "personal understanding" in comparison to the original revealed religion which Allaah sent down to our Prophet Muhammad, may the praise and salutations of Allaah be upon him. Today, meaning in the current age, we often hear in matters connected to Islaam:

- [I feel that...]
- [I have always believed...]
- [My personal view is that...]
- [In my understanding...]
- [As I see it....]
- [What I believe about that is...]
- [In my personal experience...]

...and other similar expressions which connect the religious position a person takes to their individually formed view, opinion, or perspective and not directly to the unique revealed guidance that was sent down to humanity from the Lord of the worlds, nor to the consensus of the people of knowledge throughout the centuries. Sheikh al-Islaam Ibn Taymeeyah, may Allaah have mercy upon him, said,[77]

> *"How much of what the people do is something which they wrongly have the pleasing delusion about it - that their engaging in it - is something actually from the obedience of Allaah."*

For many upon a personalized understanding of Islaam, Islaam is wrongly viewed as something which changes and naturally evolves, much like Christianity and other religions have changed and evolved over the centuries. Additionally, many Muslims today have been influenced by the modern individuals of misguidance who have innovated and distorted the reality of Islaam significantly to form a new group, party, or modern movement among Muslims. These people of innovation implicitly believe that their version of Islaam, including allegedly "good innovations", is an improvement over the Islaam of the Companions, and so is most suitable for today's Muslims. And we seek refuge in Allaah from both of these false destructive misconceptions! The end result of both approaches is that what they conceive of as Islaam is something different than what our Prophet taught and cultivated within the incredible generation of the Companions, may Allaah be pleased with them all. This is why we find that the guiding cultivating scholars from the people who adhere to the Sunnah have always stated that one of the most important needs of every Muslim is the need to properly understand their revealed religion, upon evidenced knowledge and upon clear Sharee'ah proofs, not simply based upon opinions, emotions, or limited individual perceptions or blindly followed transmission from others. This position of clarity began with the generation of the Companions and is

---

[77] Majmu'a al-Fataawa vol. 28 pg. 207

found clearly within the text of Usul as-Sunnah by Imaam Ahmad, may Allaah have mercy upon him.

Indeed the opposing false understanding of dangerously relying upon one's opinions or subjective views about a religious matter and considering that Islaam was addressed by Allaah directly in the Qur'aan. Allaah says ❧ *It is not for a believer, man or woman, when Allaah and His Messenger, have decreed a matter that they should have any option in their decision. And whoever disobeys Allaah and His Messenger, he has indeed strayed into a plain error.* ❧ – (Surah al-Ahzaab: 36) Similarly, the third righteous guided Khaleefah, 'Uthmaan Ibn 'Affaan, may Allaah the Most High be pleased with him, is reported to have said,[78]

> *"Falsehood is whatever agrees with what your desires themselves call to, even if you wrongly believe it is being done in obedience to Allaah, the Most Glorified and the Most Exalted."*

Sheikh 'Abdul-'Azeez Ibn 'Abdullah ar-Raajhee, in his commentary of this statement explained this saying,

> *"Yes, there is no doubt that this meaning is correct. Falsehood is what agrees with one's inner desires, and opposes the guidance of the source texts, even if you feel within yourself that this is an act of obedience to Allaah. Because this opinion is simply that, just one's opinion.*
>
> *As such, what is seen as falsehood is whatever agrees with one's inner desires, and opposes the source texts, even if an individual claims that the matter which his inner desires agree with should be seen as obedience to Allaah. This still remains falsehood, as the truth is whatever comes in the revealed source texts of the Book of Allaah and the Sunnah of His Messenger. Whereas falsehood is whatever agrees with your inner desires and contradicts the guidance of the source texts.*

---

[78] As narrated from al-Ibaanah al-Sughrah

Within this narration there is also found a warning against bringing new things and innovations into the religion, and a warning against the people of innovation and against listening to their doubts and claims about whatever they have innovated into Islaam. Yes."

There are many who have embraced Islaam in western countries, and in Muslim countries those who, after neglecting Islaam in their lives, have eventually recommitted themselves to living Islaam fully. Often when these Muslims are blessed to gradually grow in the authentic knowledge and understanding of our religion from the original sources of Islaam, they come to realize that much of what they initially held, or were wrongly informed was Islaam in their land, actually has no firm evidenced basis or authority from Allaah. They start to weigh and examine different religious matters found among Muslims and see that much of what others consider Islaam is not at all reflected in that Islaam which the Messenger of Allaah, may the praise and salutations of Allaah be upon him, practiced and taught.

None can deny that for modern Muslims, even after having committed themselves to following Islaam, they often hear this person's claims and that individuals' calls all confusingly made in the name of Islaam. This is caused by the fact that many of those working to promote Islaam around the world, due to various causes including their incorrect general methodology, often focus solely upon restricted aspects or areas of Islaam. The challenge we often face is trying to determine who among these different voices is correct in their claims. Some Muslim groups restrict their focus towards inward matters such as purification of the heart, while other movements focus solely on outward matters such as politics. Such groups often proceed forward with little examination or careful consideration of what specific evidence actually supports their restriction of Islaam in this unbalanced way. Whereas the correct and proper focus we must adopt is whatever is supported by the sources of Islaam as explained by the scholars standing steadfastly upon the Sunnah. Our scholars have explained that the true methodology of the Messenger of Allaah, may the praise and salutations of Allaah be upon him, was to start with that which was of primary importance and then to proceed to what was next in importance, stage by stage. Proceeding in this way, having the correct priorities at the proper time and situation leads towards achieving every goal and objective which is pleasing to Allaah, in the way directed by Allaah. This is clearly shown in the general methodology of the Messenger of Allaah throughout his life history. A failure to understand this prophetic methodology severely affects the efforts of those committed to Islaam today in many ways.

It is a sad fact that many callers among the Muslims work very hard inviting people to "Islaam", without even offering or themselves grasping a precise meaning of Islaam, as found within the original sources of revelation of our religion. Sheikh Saaleh Ibn Fauzaan al-Fauzaan, mentioned this reality stating,[79]

> *"...Additionally, regarding this general vague concept of Islaam, then is there anyone from the numerous misguided groups and sects who doesn't claim that he is upon Islaam?? Whether he is from the astray sects within the Ummah which have turned away from different aspects of the Prophet's guidance or from those radically deviant sects which have actually left the boundaries of Islaam. Each of them defines and gives Islaam a customized and tailored meaning according to their own views and positions, methodology and way.*

---

[79] 'Eanaat al-Mustafeed Bee Sharh Kitaab at-Tawheed by Sheikh Saaleh Fauzaan: page 208

> *The name 'Islaam', has become a cape or covering garment claimed and worn by every misguided astray sect from among the ranks of the Muslims as well as those radically deviant sects which have in fact apostated from Islaam- whether this is the Qadiyaneeyah, the Baatineeyah generally, those groups who worship at graves, or others."*

Consider a common example of this *"general vague concept of Islaam"* where many people have their own deficient personalized versions of Islaam, all with differing, if not openly contradictory, beliefs and practices. Throughout the Ummah, some general Muslims claiming to worship Allaah alone also wrongly supplicate, sacrifice, and donate money, food, and wealth at the grave sites of the dead righteous Muslims who are in their graves, seeking a reward and hoping for intercession with Allaah, just as Christians do with their dead righteous whom they consider saints! Yet, our beloved messenger taught us that Allaah will never accept that from us. The Companion of the Prophet, 'Abdul-Hameed bin Ja'far narrated in an authentic hadeeth,[80]

> *"My father informed me, from Ibn Mina, from Abu Sa'eed bin Abee Fadalah al-Ansari - and he was one of the Companions - who said: 'I heard the Messenger of Allaah said:*
>
> *{When Allaah gathers the people on the Day of Judgement - a Day in which there is no doubt in - a caller will call out: 'Whoever took an associate with others in any of his deeds he did for Allaah - then let him seek his reward from that other than Allaah. For indeed Allaah is the most free of the partners from any need of anything which has been directed to other than Him alone.}*

This serious sin and grave error strikes at the very heart or

---
[80] Jaame'a' at-Tirmidhee, no: 3448

what is and what is not Islaam, and what Allaah will accept or reject from us on that Day of Reckoning, a day which there is no doubt about. Despite this, in this current state of confusion some Muslims, without evidence, falsely believe that all of these differences which we have come to see, including supplicating to the righteous dead in their graves just as one supplicates to Allaah, the Most High, should all be blindly accepted and considered part of the religion of Islaam. By Allaah's mercy, Allaah's Messenger gave us specific guidance of how to approach and deal with the trial of emergence of the many differences among the Muslims which would occur after him, as mentioned in the hadeeth of al-'Irbaadh Ibn Saareeyah who said: [81]

> *{...I have left you upon clear guidance, its night is like its day; no one deviates from it except one who is destroyed. And whoever lives for some time from amongst you will see great differing; so stick to what you know from my Sunnah and the Sunnah of the rightly guided caliphs...}*

This guiding hadeeth in and of itself is a strong indication the perfection of the guidance given to our beloved Messenger, may the praise and salutations of Allaah be upon him, which he taught and conveyed to his Ummah completely. It is his guiding Sunnah which gives us that detailed knowledge and those clarifying descriptions needed to distinguish between the many conflicting positions among the Muslims, since every differing Muslim sect or group claims that what they believe and practice is truly from Islaam. It is the clarifying sunnah

---

[81] Narrated through various narrations in Sunan Abu Dawud: 4607/ Jaame' al-Tirmidhee: 2676/ Sunan Ibn Maajah: 42, 43, 45/ & Musnad of Imaam Ahmad: 16692, 16693, 16695/ -on the authority of al-'Irbaadh Ibn Saareeyah. It was declared authentic by Sheikh al-Albaanee in Silsilat al-Hadeeth as-Saheehah: 937, (his verification of) Mishkaat al-Masaabeh: 165, Saheeh at-Targheeb at-Tarheeb: 37, Dhelaal al-Jannah: 33, 45, as-Saheeh al-Jaame'a' as-Sagheer: 2539, 4369, as well as in others of his books. Sheikh Muqbil declared it authentic in al-Jaame'a' al-Saheeh: 3249, and he did not state any difference with the ruling of authenticity given by Haafidh al-Haakim in his own verification of al-Mustadrak alaa Saheehayn- 'Pursuing the Errors of al-Haakim which adh-Dhahaabee Did Not Mention' regarding hadeeth numbers 329, 331, 332

of the rightly guided caliphs which gives us that further knowledge and a practical example of how to adhere to the Sunnah when those differences actually emerge among the Muslims. As indeed every differing Muslim sect or group claims that what they believe and practice is truly from Islaam. He, may the praise and salutations of Allaah be upon him, specifically described those guided Muslim remaining upon his original guidance as those who would always be present through time, in every century. Likewise, he, may the praise and salutations of Allaah be upon him, specifically described some of those who would turn away from and deviate from his Sunnah and the straight path of Allaah.

This tremendous confusion caused by every sect claiming to be upon Islaam generally is the reason our scholars have stated that one aspect of the correct methodology of Islaam includes constantly defending and clarifying what actually was the original Islaam of our beloved Prophet upon evidences and clear proofs. A second important aspect is continually educating and cultivating the Muslims upon that affirmed body of evidenced knowledge and correct practices.

Sheikh Zayd al-Madkhalee, may Allaah have mercy upon him, stated in his writing, 'The Well Established Principles of the Way of the First Generations of Muslims: It's Enduring & Excellent Distinct Characteristics' that,

> *"...From among these principles and characteristics is that the methodology of tasfeeyah -or clarification- and tarbeeyah -or education and cultivation- is clearly affirmed and established as a true way coming from the first three generations of Islaam, and is something well known to the people of true merit from among them, as is concluded by considering all the related evidence.*
>
> *What is intended by tasfeeyah, when referring to it generally, is clarifying that which is the truth from that*

which is falsehood, what is goodness from that which is harmful and corrupt, and when referring to its specific meanings it is distinguishing the noble Sunnah of the Prophet and the people of the Sunnah from those innovated matters brought into the religion and the people who are supporters of such innovations.

As for what is intended by tarbeeyah, it is calling all of the creation to take on the manners and embrace the excellent character invited to by that guidance revealed to them by their Lord through His worshiper and Messenger Muhammad, may Allaah's praise and salutations be upon him; so that they might have good character, manners, and behavior. As without this they cannot have a good life, nor can they put right their present condition or their final destination. And we seek refuge in Allaah from the evil of not being able to achieve that rectification."

As some scholars have pointed out, many Muslim sects, groups, and movements dislike this focus of clarifying and seeking clarity of the beliefs and practices of Islaam from its original sources. They dislike the scholars' refutations that come forward due to their own inability to support and defend their own false claims which they have wrongly attached to Islaam, when weighed against those original sources and original people of truth. Such Muslims not only fail to see the tremendous value and clarity of us using the authentic essential descriptions found in authentic hadeeth narrations which our beloved Messenger himself gave us as Muslims, but vigorously oppose it. Yet these descriptions, and the terms related to them, only guide the sincere Muslims towards good and towards being steadfast and away from that misguidance Shaytaan desires for us and his aim of our going astray. Sheikh Muhammad Ibn 'Umar Baazmool, explains some of the benefits of these descriptive terms in our interactions with others, guiding the one who asks with sincerity in order to understand this issue. [82]

> It has been said, [I want to speak to you about something. Why do you use the term 'the saved sect'? Why do you chose to call yourselves something other than 'Muslims'? Why would you choose to also use another name like 'Salafee' for example!]

> I responded: One can use the general term "Muslim" when they dealing with a non-Muslims. But when you are interacting with other Muslims, such as someone who commonly follows his own thoughts and ideas and gives precedence to intellectual conclusions above all else, then in this situation you should distinguish yourself as a Muslim proceeding distinctly from that persons's own misguided way. This is by saying for example: I am a Muslim who is Atharee, meaning a Muslim following the body of transmitted knowledge from the first generations, not simply relying upon or giving preference to my own or another's intellectual conclusions.

> Likewise, if there is a Shee'ah Raafidhee deceptively claiming and attaching himself to Islaam, then one would say, in order to distinguish yourself from him by saying "I am a Sunnee Muslim.", meaning I believe in the excellence and high merit of the Companions of the Messenger of Allaah.

> In this way you provide a needed additional clarifying description along with your general attribution to Islaam in order to clearly distinguish yourself from those who also attribute themselves to Islaam generally, but who at the same time, along with the broad attribution, proceeds upon some incorrect methodology that is not supported by the evidenced truth of Islaam's guidance.

---

[82] From the Facebook page of Sheikh Muhammad Ibn 'Umar Baazmool 11-06-17

In our current age, the descriptive term, Salafeeyah, has come to be used to distinguish the people upon the Sunnah as a whole, distinct from the people of innovation who are following their desires, as well as from the different so called "Islamic" parties and groups found within the Muslim Ummah. Such that one says, " I am a Salafee Muslim," meaning I do not connect myself to any of the various groups or Muslim parties. Rather I strive to adhere to and stand upon what the Messenger of Allaah, may Allaah's praise and salutations be upon him, and his Companions, stood upon originally.

If we were suppose hypothetically, for the sake of discussion, that the Muslims were to truly abandon and turn away from all these different methodologies and devised perspectives, then and only in that actual situation would we have not have any need to say anything other than: "I am Muslim.", which, by itself would in that case sufficiently distinguishes someone from the disbelievers. And the success is from Allaah."

Within the text of Usul as-Sunnah, Imaam Ahmad accurately indicates who is considered from the people properly and truly adhering to the Sunnah, using a descriptive name and related characteristics. Correspondingly, he also points out what distinguishing characteristics are found among the people of misguidance, those who are outside the boundaries of the Sunnah and proceed upon an innovated methodology which is wrongly connected to Islaam. These descriptive terms have been used by the verifying scholars throughout the history of our Muslim Ummah to indicate that there is a right way and numerus wrong ways of understanding and practicing Islaam when viewed in light of the Qur'aan and Sunnah an their established principles.

As some of the people of knowledge have stated, there are some Muslims who do not understand why indicating the details of how someone proceeds in their beliefs and actions is important at all. Many do not understand what is the meant by this idea of methodology or the general way a Muslim lives Islaam, and are confused by the Arabic term used for methodology- minhaj. Some dislike the term methodology due to what its acceptance must lead to of clarifying distinguishing people's separation from the guidance within the source texts in the different areas of the guidance of Islaam. In our modern age, this separation is often due to the misplaced objective of partisan Muslim groups and movements of seeking unity among Muslims at any cost, by any means, and upon any understanding.

The following question itself is an important example related to firstly, the importance of taking the correct evidenced beliefs of Islaam from the scholars, and secondly, being aware of common distorted perceptions that oppose the Sunnah, even though people are so attached to them. Sheikh 'Abdul-Muhsin al-'Abaad, may Allaah preserve him, was asked, [83] ***"We have heard your statement about the term minhaj or methodology, that it is accepted in accordance to what it is connected to. But what is your view of the one who claims [This term is a newly invented expression and so it in impermissible to use it.]?"*** He replied,

> *"How could this term be considered something newly invented? As it is found in the language of the Arabs, and it has a clear sound meaning in the Arabic language? So it is accepted according to what it is attached to in its use. As for methodology generally, then indeed every person has one, with that being what they put in place and fully accept for themselves in their affairs. If the methodology they have adopted is correct then it is the correct methodology. And if their methodology contains falsehood, then it is a false methodology.*

---

[83] From the questions and answers of his explanation of Sunan Abu Dawud - Kitab al-Jihad

For this reason it is said, the methodology of the people of the Sunnah and adherence to the Jamaa'ah in the area of beliefs is such-and-such meaning from positions and principles, and that their methodology in actions and endeavors is similarly this way and that way. As their methodology is their general path, way and approach. Meaning that their path in determining the matters of beliefs of Islaam is that they rely and base them upon the revealed source texts and transmitted knowledge, and that they do not rely and base them upon our intellects and the conclusions they reach. For them intellectual conclusion must be subservient and conform to transmitted knowledge from the source texts. Such that their intellectual views do not oppose what has been transmitted from revealed knowledge.

Therefore about this term methodology, one cannot correctly say it is newly invented and should not be used. Rather, its meaning is correct and sound, however it is used and taken according to what matter it is connected and referring to. As every sect has a specific methodology, every group or movement has a specific methodology and a particular path it proceeds upon. This is simply the reality, as such there is no danger in its use."

Our verifying scholars past and present state that every separate group or sect has a distinct methodology, usually coming from its original leader or founder upon falsehood, and then often further changed and altered by those coming after them, so what then distinguishes the correct methodology of Islaam? What focus and which important fundamentals that the Prophet himself proceeded upon did he guide us to? Why do those guided Muslims in every century, who love his Sunnah, strive and struggle to stand upon the same methodology as the first Muslims? Sheikh Saaleh as-Suhaymee, may Allaah preserve him, in response to a question, makes clear that the correct methodology is everything related to establishing the essential foundation of Islaam itself which is truly worshiping Allaah alone in every way, [84]

> *"The progressive cultivating methodology of the Prophet encompasses beliefs and other matters beyond that. Indeed it includes everything which he, may Allaah's praise and salutations be upon him, was upon as well as that which his Companions were upon.*
>
> *From the direction of aqeedah or beliefs: it is the correct belief that Allaah alone is to be worshipped upon which we base our allegiance and disassociation with people, and which is a realization of that subservience to Allaah the Most Exalted, the Most Magnificent. It is the realization of worshipping Allaah alone in regards to abandoning those outward actions of associating others along with him and idolatry, and it is the realization of the statement that there is none worthy of worship other than Allaah, and believing this to mean that there is none truly worthy and deserving of worship in truth other than Allaah.*
>
> *What is intended is that each Muslim make this a reality and strives in this matter of Allaah's worship alone such that the beneficial causes of success which Allaah has decreed are brought forth. He strives until that final time comes when the obligations and duties of this life are removed from him after he has successfully established the worship of Allaah, the Most Exalted, the Most High."*

---

[84] Question 234 from the Second collection of Ruling from Sh. Saaleh as-Suhaymee.

Sheikh Hammad Ibn Muhammad al-Ansaaree, may Allaah have mercy upon him, insightfully said about the age we currently live in, [85]

> *"This age and century is characterized as being one of open rebellion against Allaah, the Most Glorified and the Most Exalted, and His guidance."*

Sheikh Muhammad Ibn Saaleh al-'Utheimeen, may Allaah have mercy upon him, said,[86]

> *"Those who oppose the truth are of two types of people,[87] the first type openly admit that opposition, and clearly understand that they are opposing what is correct. His situation is very clear to everyone.*
>
> *The second type is the person who is too arrogant to accept the truth, and he tends to distort and falsely interpret the source texts in order to support his desires and whims. This second type is much more dangerous to Islaam than the first type, due to the fact that he puts forward the outward pretense of following the guidance of Islaam, yet in reality he is not from those people actually submitting to that guidance- even to a degree."*

The guiding scholar Sheikh Saaleh Ibn Fauzaan, may Allaah preserve him, said,[88]

> *"Today, deception and lying is something widespread among people, such that someone who wants to advance some statement or position just attributes it to someone accepted so that it will be accepted by others."*

---

[85] al-Majmu'a from the Biography of Sheikh Hammaad Ibn Muhammad al-Ansaaree pg. 585
[86] Tafseer of the Surah al-Baqarah by Sheikh al-'Utheimeen, may Allaah have mercy upon him
[87] Refer to Course Appendix 1: Leaving The Straight Way Occurs In Two Ways- in the book ' 30 Day Of Guidance: Book 1'
[88] From a lesson in the series 'Explanation of the Book Fath al-Majeed' held on 04-23-1437

This is important to realize when is comes to examining our sources of knowledge, which is a core objective of this initial course book, seeking knowledge of Islaam, and considering the various callers to Islaam. The guiding scholar Sheikh Saaleh Ibn Fauzaan, may Allaah preserve him, said, [89]

"The truth is not something reached by intellectual endeavors, nor by looking to the common customs of people, nor through generally blind following someone, nor through various devised concepts and ideas. The truth is something which is only reached through turning to revelation from Allaah."

Sheikh al-'Utheimeen, may Allaah, the Most High, have mercy upon him, also said about inward intentions, seeking knowledge, and the deficiencies of the people involved in innovation related to them both,[90]

"How pervasive is the evil intention related to knowledge of the religion, which is found among the people of innovation. As some of them insist upon, and persist stubbornly upon misguidance even after the evidenced truth of what they proceed upon has been made clear to them.

Indeed, the causes for someone having a deficiency in knowledge of the religion are four:

Firstly: lacking in the knowledge one possesses

Secondly: a shortcoming in properly seeking out knowledge

Thirdly: a failure to fully understand the knowledge one does possesses

---

[89] Explanation of the hadeeth "We were previously in the time of Jaahileeyah..." pg. 15

[90] Sharh Taqreeb at-Tadroomeeyah: pg 389

Fourthly: having evil or bad intention in relation to the knowledge."

One of the errors a Muslim may fall into that may be considered having a bad intention towards knowledge is simply seeking knowledge to discover whatever supports the concepts, ideas, and personal views he already holds, as Sheikh al-'Utheimeen mentioned, *"...he tends to distort and falsely interpret the source texts in order to support his desires and whims..."* This dangerous way is followed by many rather than the correct way of generally turning to the sources of revelation humbly and sincerely to find what guidance they have for the worshiper of Allaah and then forming one's positions and stances based upon that preserved perfect guidance after investigation or asking the people of knowledge. This is often caused by a person generally giving precedence to, and going beyond the bounds regarding the proper use of the blessing of their human intellect. He, Sheikh Hammad al-Ansaaree may Allaah have mercy upon him, advised that, [91]

"The diseases of the heart are of two types, misconceptions and desires. The sickness of misconceptions can reach disbelief, whereas the sickness of desires is a grave sin.

As for misconceptions, then people of the Sunnah hold that it is not allowed to mention (what is unknown) of them in front of the general Muslims, nor others for fear that in bringing them forward that may negatively affect the hearts of those present."

What is presented here is not all of the doubts called to by those who have chosen to who give precedence to their intellect in judging and understanding the source texts of Islaam, but only some of those which the scholars have clarified and addressed due to their presence among many people. The guiding scholar Sheikh Saaleh Ibn Fauzaan,

[91] Al-Majmu'a from the Biography of Sheikh Hammaad Ibn Muhammad al-Ansaaree: Number 222

may Allaah preserve him, said,[92]

> *"Those people upon the way of falsely understanding the religion, through the misguided desires they hold, wish to separate and distance themselves from those authentic affirmed evidences within the Sharee'ah. This is in order that nothing opposes them in following their own devised ideas and concepts."*

This corrupting way and practice of selectively choosing according to one's intellect is not something new but was also found among those misguided people who, in the first centuries of Islaam, turned away from the correct methodology of the believers way. Ayyoob as-Sakhteeyaanee said,[93]

> *"If you speak to a man about the guidance of the Sunnah, and he responds, [We should leave this, sufficient for us is the Qur'aan.] Then know that is he someone misguided and astray."*

One of the central features of the tremendous work Usul as-Sunnah is Imaam Ahmad's effective clarification and his refutation of the misapplication and misuse of the human intellect as an equivalent source for determining what are correct beliefs and practices an individual should adopt to be successful as a Muslim. Imaam Ahmad, may Allaah have mercy upon him, distinguishes the balanced guidance of the Prophet and that of his esteemed Companions, from the false way of reliance upon the results of solitary intellect efforts and arbitrary derived conclusions or selective misapplication of source texts, saying,

> *9. There are no purely intellectual analogies in the Sunnah nor are speculative examples from it.*

---

[92] Explanation of the hadeeth "We were previously in the time of Jaahileeyah..." pg. 31
[93] Dham al-Kalaam Narration # 216

10. Its guidance is not something fully comprehended by someone's intellect nor agreeing with someone's fanciful whims or inclinations.

11. Rather it is affirmation and following, and turning away from following one's whims and inclinations in the religion.

He also states, within the text of Usul as-Sunnah, an important guideline that distinguishes incorrect methodologies which commonly misuse the intellect, even if perchance the correct conclusion is somehow reached,

21. The one who engages in this way of rhetorical debates, even if he arrives at the truth through his statements, he is not from the people who follow the Sunnah until he abandons using this way, and submits and truly believes in the sound transmitted narrations.

These proper boundaries of the role of the human intellect in Islaam are made very clear by the early and later scholars upon the Sunnah. Sheikh Hammaad Ibn Muhammad al-Ansaaree, may Allaah, the Most High have mercy upon him, said,[94]

"The disbelievers have a single intellectual sphere of activity, but we have two: one related to our using and benefiting from the material world and one related to properly using our intellects within the revealed Sharee'ah."

Al-Hasan al-Basree explained the self-reproach needed from the Muslim who wrongfully allows his intellect to overstep the proper boundaries and its rightful place, when he said,[95]

"Blame and reproach your own desires and opinions for

---

[94] al-Majmu'a from the Biography of Sheikh Hammaad Ibn Muhammad al-Ansaaree pg. 576

[95] al-Madkhal illa as-Sunnan al-Kubraa of Imaam al-Bayhaqee : Chapter on the Criticism of Opinion and the Unsuitability of Using Analogies in the presence of a Sound source text Hadeeth 159

being astray whenever they are given precedence over the clear guidance of the religion of Allaah and then sincerely advise and direct yourself and your practices of Islaam to accept being guided by the guidance of the Book of Allaah."

Ibn al-Qayyim, may Allaah have mercy upon him, explained that being blessed to knowingly submit to revelation fully, which includes restricting the use of our intellects to the proper limits, and proceeding upon that with steadfastness, is one of the foundations of true success in our lives as Muslims,[96]

"When a worshiper of Allaah is blessed to be someone who submits in compliance with the truth, and is granted steadfastness upon it, then they should have glad tidings, since they have been blessed in every general area. This only occurs through the favor of Allaah which He gives to whomever He chooses."

Sheikh Saaleh Ibn Fauzaan, may Allaah preserve him, explained the clear criterion for proving one's required love of Allaah,[97]

"The person who claims that he truly loves Allaah, yet turns away from following and adhering to the guidance of the Messenger, upon him be Allaah's praise and salutations, is someone who is not sincere and truthful in this claim he is making of loving Him."

He, may Allaah preserve him, also warned against blindly following the conclusions, opinions, and positions taken by people who are well known, yet are whose positions not actually based upon evidenced guidance,[98]

"A Muslim must strongly prevent himself from being someone who calls to that which is wrong and from the

---

[96] Turuq al-Hijratayn: vol. 2 pg. 347
[97] From the lecture 'The Causes for a Worshiper of Allaah Gaining the Love of Allaah' given on 01-18-1432
[98] Explanation of the Structured Poem al-Ha'eeyah: pg. 107

adherence to desires regardless of whoever accepts and promotes this matter of misguidance from among the people, no matter who they are."

Sheikh al-Islaam Ibn Taymeeyah, may Allaah have mercy upon him, said,[99]

"Following your desires in matters of the religion is more dangerous and more serious than simply following your desires in worldly wants and pleasures."

Sheikh Muhammad Ibn 'Umar Baazmool, was asked, [100] **Question: It is found in the book Iqtidhaa' al-'Ilm al-'Amal by Khateeb al-Baghdaadee that some of the people of knowledge from the first three generations said, "With manners, you will come to understand knowledge." What is the correct explanation of their statement?**

Answer: Yes, this expression is part of a narration found in the book Iqtidhaa' al-'Ilm al-'Amal by Khateeb al-Baghdaadee, page thirty-one: Yusuf Ibn al-Husayn said, "With good manners, you will come to understand knowledge, and through knowledge you are able to rectify your deeds, through performing your deeds you are able to acquire wisdom, and through gaining wisdom you'll come to understand the meaning of abstinence for Allaah's sake from the harmful matters in worldly life and successfully cultivating this, and through such abstinence of matters harmful to your Hereafter you will turn away from seeking temporary success in this world, and through turning away from seeking temporary success in this world one gains the desire for lasting success in the Hereafter, and through the desire to gain true success in the Hereafter, one achieves the pleasure of Allaah, the Most Glorified and the Most Exalted."

---

[99] The Treatise Enjoining the Good and forbidding evil. pg. 9
[100] Question and Answer 319: from the sheikh's website

So I say: The good manners through which someone is blessed to understand knowledge have several angles or perspectives: having good manners with Allaah the Most Perfect and the Most High, having good manners with His Messenger, may Allaah's praise and salutations be upon him, having good manners with the Companions, may Allaah be please with all of them, and having good manners with the scholars, may Allaah have mercy upon them, both those who are living in those that have died.

Such that if a person acts with good manners with Allaah and His Messenger, then he will never give precedence to his own opinion over any statement of Allaah or any statement of His Messenger, rather he will accept and rely upon what is directed to by these source texts.

Furthermore, this includes implementing these matters according to what also comes from the understanding first generations of Islaam. So we understand the Qur'aan and the hadeeth narrations upon the same methodology and way that the first righteous generations did, and also following the correct understandings found within the statements of the scholars who themselves follow and adhere to the way of the righteous first generations. Those scholars are the inheritors of the Prophets, so found with them and only with them is the correct understanding of Sharee'ah knowledge, taken from the sources of guidance.

As for the one who does not act with good manners with Allaah and His Messenger, he is someone who gives precedence to his own intellectual conclusions, opinions, and desires above the word of Allaah and the statements of the Messenger of Allaah, and in this way he forbids himself from truly understanding knowledge. He is not able to, nor will he ever be able to understand it until Allaah guides him to what is correct in submitting to guidance truly.

Similarly, when someone abandons what is found among the Companions of the Messenger of Allaah, and treats it like something which is thrown behind their back, then they become similar to the astray sects of the Shee'ah, the Khawaarij, the Jahmeeyah, the Mu'tazilah, and those intellectuals who falsely rely upon their intellects for guidance, and whoever is similar to them. They all reject what comes from the Companions generally, and they do not look to it nor turn their faces towards their sound understanding. Such a person has also forbidden themselves from truly understanding knowledge, he is not able and he will never be able to understand it until Allaah guides him to what is correct.

Furthermore, if as part of lacking good manners, you do not refer back to the statements of the well-known reliable people of knowledge and do not have a good suspicion about them, you fail to prevent yourself from being someone who quickly thinks poorly of them, jumps to refute them by leaping forward with your own personal thinking, thrusting your understanding and your intellectual conclusions ahead of the scholars, so twisting the source texts to conform to your desires and whatever you want in trying to explain the Qur'aan and the Sunnah. Then you are someone who has clearly turned away from the true wellspring of knowledge, and brought yourself to the edge of the pit of following misleading desires, except if Allaah guides you to accept what is correct. This is what is intended by this saying, and Allaah knows best."

Sheikh Sulaymaan ar-Ruhaylee, may Allaah preserve him, explained the proper way for the Muslim who is seeking knowledge for the purpose of properly worship Allaah,[101]

"As for the student of knowledge when he comes to know about a certain issue or matter that it is an issue which

---

[101] From his series Explanation of al-Waseeyat ul-Kubraa within the eighth lesson

the guided Muslims of the Ummah have come to stand in agreement upon, then know it is the truth. As for when the issue is one that the people of guidance have differed about, then look into it and consider.

If the matter in which they are differing about is due to a specific incident or current event, then look to see if before that event was there previously a difference or were the people unified in that issue? If before this occurrence of differing there was unity among the guided Muslims then that position of unity is what you should hold firmly to, that unified position which existed in the first period of the Ummah. As that is the truth, that some of the people later become disconnected and separated from.

If there comes forward a disputed matter related to the correct fundamental beliefs of Islaam and we find that the first three generations agreed in their understanding of a matter, and then at a later time the people came to differ about it, in this case we should not have any hesitation or need to consider the possibilities, rather the clear truth certainly is whatever position the first Muslim generations of this Ummah agreed upon, meaning in the original and early period of Islaam. Correspondingly, falsehood is whatever came about later as something separated from and differing from what the first generations agreed upon.

If, in the case of the issue being considered, there was no previous position agreed upon among the Muslims before that differing began, then look and consider which of the positions is supported by anything transmitted from the evidences of the source texts. If you find that one of the stated positions is supported by transmitted evidences then hold firmly to that supported position, and turn away from whatever opposes it.

This last situation is what is referred to by the meaning of the statement of the scholars of jurisprudence, when discussing the derivation of rulings, when they say "Independent scholastic reasoning is not used or considered when there is a clear relevant source text present." This is also the meaning of the statement of Imaam ash-Shaafa'ee, "The people stand in consensus that whoever it becomes clear and evident to that there is an affirmed Sunnah of Messenger of Allaah, may Allaah's praise and salutations be upon him, then is not acceptable for him to turn away from that Sunnah in order to accept the statement of anyone from among the people, no matter who that person may be in status and understanding."

Moreover if the issue which the people are differing about is found not to be firstly one in which there was previously unity regarding, nor secondly an issue in which there appears to be any relevant evidence which supports and strengthens one of the various positions, and the differing statements remain as something which confuses the student of knowledge considering them, then he should ask and supplicate to Allaah for guidance. He should ask his Lord to inspire him and grant him the understanding of the truth which the people have differed about.

It is for this specific reason that in this text al-Waseeyat ul-Kubraa, the sheikh, Sheikh al-Islaam Ibn Taymeeyah, says, "If you are confused about a matter which the people have differed regarding, then supplicate to Allaah with the supplication which was narrated by Imaam Muslim in his Saheeh on the authority of 'A'ishah, may Allaah be pleased with her, that Messenger of Allaah, may Allaah's praise and salutations be upon him, when he got up at night to pray, from the opening supplications with which he, the Prophet, would begin his night prayer with was:

[Oh Allaah, Lord of Gabriel, and Mikaa'el, and Israafeel, the Creator of the heavens and the earth, Who knows the unseen and the seen; You decide among Your servants concerning the matters they have differences in. Guide me to what is the truth with, by Your permission, in the divergent views which the people hold. For it is You Who guides whom You will to the Straight Path.] [102]"

This balanced and proper use of the intellect, between neglect and misapplication, is a hallmark of the saved sect among the astray sects of the Ummah. It is a characteristic which distinguishes those who remained on the truth and followed the Jamaa'ah. Accordingly, the correct and evidenced meaning of the Jamaa'ah being that group of Muslims, starting with the Companions, may Allaah be pleased with them all, who affirm and proceed upon everything the Last Messenger who was sent to humanity taught his noble Companions as Islaam.

---

[102] Saheeh Muslim:770

YOUR GOAL WHEN STUDYING[103]

Whenever we start any action or begin any effort in which we ask Allaah to bless us in, such as undertaking a course to further study and learn our religion, we must make sure our effort conforms with the comprehensive methodology of our beloved Prophet in only seeking the pleasure of Allaah- inwardly and outwardly. Beginning such an endeavor holds tremendous amounts of potential good for us as Muslims and the opportunity to come closer to Allaah and everything Allaah loves and is pleased with. We must remember that Allaah, the Most High, said,[104]

{Oh son of Aadam - when you step forward towards Me then I proceed forward towards you, and when you come walking towards Me then I hasten towards you.}

To truly move closer to Allaah we first need a foundation of understanding and knowledge of what we are aiming for. Sheikh Bakr Abu Zayd, may Allaah have mercy upon him, has mentioned in his work Hukm al-Intima'a,

> *"The removal of the shadow of ignorance is accomplished through the light of knowledge of this religion which we have inherited from the Prophet, may Allaah's praise and salutations be upon him. For this reason Imaam al-Bukhaaree, may Allaah the Most high, have mercy upon him, stated in the Book of knowledge within his work Saheeh al-Bukhaaree, as chapter heading "The Chapter Of Knowledge Coming Before Statement And Deed". And when you have acquired knowledge, this then requires that you act and that you realize four different objectives:*
>
> *a- The rectification of your thinking, understanding, and beliefs*

---

[103] Amended from original introduction
[104] Silsilaat al-Hadeeth as-Saheehah:2287 with an authentic chain as found in the Musnad of Imaam Ahmad

b- The rectification of your actions and deeds

c- The development of that personal restraint which is born from the self respect possessed by the knowledgable Muslim which prevents him from the unwarily stumbling into error within ones thoughts, conceptions..."

One of the defining characteristics of the original text of Usul as-Sunnah is the attention it gives to distinguishing between the different practices or methods of understanding, and to clarifying the details and characteristics of the correct methodology which conforms to the guidance of the Prophet without any change or alteration. This true methodology is that single distinct clear way which Allaah has preserved for this Ummah, as a beacon of guidance remaining bright until the Day of Judgement. Sheikh Muhammad Khaleel Harraas, may Allaah have mercy upon him, states in his explanation of Aqeedah al-Waaseteeyah,[105]

*" The author stated, "**Then from the way of the people of the Sunnah...**" To the end of his words.*

This statement clarifies the methodology of the people who adhere to the Sunnah and the Jamaa'ah in deriving the rulings and guidelines of the entire religion, both its fundamentals and its subsidiary matters, after the author has previously indicated their way and methodology in specific fundamental issues. Their methodology is based upon three source foundations:

Firstly, the Book of Allaah, Glorified and Exalted, which is the best and most truthful of speech. They do not give precedence to the statements of anyone over the Speech of Allaah, the Qur'aan.

---

[105] Sharh al-Aqeedah al-Waaseteyyah: pg. 256-257

Secondly, the Sunnah of the Messenger of Allaah, may Allaah's praise and salutations be upon him, that which is transmitted from him of his guidance and his way. Similarly, they do not give precedence or a position of preference to the statements of anyone over the Sunnah.

And thirdly, acceptance of those matters which the people of the first period of Muslim Ummah have agreed upon and united upon in consensus before the separations and divisions began to spread and innovation in the religion, various false claims, and misguiding statements began to appear among the Muslims.

Whatever comes to them, to those people who adhere to the Sunnah and the Jamaa'ah, from the statements which people follow from various claims and assertions - they weigh and assess them upon these three foundations: the Qur'aan, Sunnah, and Ijma'a. If those assertions conform to the guidance of these sources then they accept them, and if they differ with these sources they reject and turn away from them, no matter who is the one who stated it.

This is the balanced methodology, and the straight path which the one who proceeds upon it is preserved from going astray, and the one who follows it never can be wretched. It is the middle path between those who play with and twist the source texts, distorting the meaning of the Book of Allaah, denying what is found in authentic narrations, and give no consideration to what the first generation united upon as Islaam, and between the one who speaks haphazardly and recklessly, legitimizing every opinion, and accepting every statement, not distinguishing between what has the substance of truth and what is worthless, between that which is correct and that which is false."

It is important to note that the Usul as-Sunnah course book is for the individual who is sincerely seeking to study Islaam from:

1. Its original two revealed sources of the Qur'aan and the Sunnah
2. The vast scholastic body of knowledge produced throughout the centuries produced by the reliable scholars of the victorious saved group that reflects and explains those sources of revelation

By this meaning those essential inward beliefs and outward practices reflected within that group of Muslims that our Messenger, may Allaah's praise and salutations be upon him, stated explicitly would remain upon his preserved guidance in every century and every age starting with the noble Companions, may Allaah be pleased with them all and increase us in our love of them.

The selection of the preeminent work 'Usul as-Sunnah' as the foundation of this course is not related in any way to some imagined need to return to an earlier time, as often claimed by those who fail to grasp the essential nature and foundations of the way of understanding Islaam according to the model and established methodology of the first generations of Islaam. Rather its choice was because the distinction this text has of embodying those correct beliefs and that sound balanced methodology which form the core of the single divinely revealed path of guidance. It was produced by a preeminent distinctive scholar who was acknowledged by the entire Ummah to be a deep ocean of knowledge of Islaam, in both its principles and actual realized daily practice, upon adherence to the Sunnah. His position and status was acknowledged across the lands of the Muslims, so much so that even his funeral was distinguished and remarkable.

Sheikh al-Islaam Ibn Taymeeyah, may Allaah have mercy upon him, said,[106]

> *"Islaam had never seen in its history the likes of his funeral, meaning Ahmad Ibn Hanbal."*

For these reasons it is important to address a possible misunderstanding the reader might have. Some may call the work of Usul as-Sunnah a reflection of the beliefs of Ahmad Ibn Hanbal. This generalization, which although correct in one aspect, may reflect a common misunderstanding, which may be fostered by people's separation from referring to the revealed source texts, that Islaam is connected to the beliefs held by this one person or that specific individual. But this is not correct, except in the context of this or that person truly reflecting and affirming the original beliefs found in the noble Qur'aan, authentic Sunnah, and what the Ummah stands in Consensus upon. As those seeking knowledge, from the very first step we undertake to learn the beliefs of Islaam, we must be aware that these are not the beliefs of any one person only but that the author as a scholar, only reflected the revealed guidance which reached them. As Sheikh Muhammad Ibn 'Abdul-Hameed al-Hassuna, may Allaah have mercy upon him, mentioned,[107]

> *"The questioner asserts that he has accepted knowledge from one of his brothers and established his final position upon the methodology of so-and so in beliefs! So I say before anything else, it is unquestionably acknowledged that our beliefs do not originate from any individual, rather they follow what is transmitted in the revealed source texts, just as was mentioned by Sheikh al-Islaam Ibn Taymeeyah, may Allaah have mercy upon him...."*

---

[106] al-Intisaar Ahlul-Athaar, of Ibn Taymeeyah, pg. 16
[107] Muhammad Ibn Abdul-Hameed Hasunna in "Hawee al-Hawaa" 8/21/143

Furthermore the sheikh, may Allaah have mercy upon him, also mentioned,[108]

> "...And these beliefs are the first and foremost obligation up the worshipper of Allaah. Through them his heart is corrected and he establishes the foundation of following guidance, your general understanding become straightforward, and the person is uplifted by it. Just as through negligence of it or opposing something of the correct beliefs, what is brought about is personal audacity and recklessness towards a clear text of guidance, or its people, as well as the slipping into innovation and the changing of the religion of Islaam."

Specifically describing the important distinguishing positions within the text of Usul as-Sunnah, such as affirming that the Qur'aan as uncreated, as-Safaareenee said, [109]

> "That position which Ahmad held was held by all the previous leading scholars, even if some of them had more knowledge of it than others, were stronger in explaining it, bringing it forth, and defending falsehood in relation to it."

Abu Dawood as-Sijinstaanee stated, reflecting that these beliefs were held by the other well known scholars upon the Sunnah at that time, in his collection of issues asked of Imaam Ahmad, [110]

> "I heard Ishaaq Ibn Ibraheem being asked about the people who professed that their own recitation was created, and he declared them to be those upon innovation."

---

[108] Muhammad Ibn Abdul-Hameed Hasunna in "Hawee al-Hawaa" 8/21/143
[109] Lawaama' al-'Anwaar, pg 74
[110] Masa'il Ahmad (Statements on Issues by Imaam Ahmad) narrated by Abu Dawood as-Sijinstaanee, pg 217

Similarly, Imaam at-Tabaree narrated that two of the leading scholars in the hadeeth science of commending and criticizing narrators, Abu Zur'ah 'Ubayd Ibn 'Abdul-Kareem ar-Raazee, and Abu Haatim Muhammad Ibn Idrees ar-Raazee, both said,[111]

> *"The one who professes [My recitation of the Qur'aan] is created is from the sect of the Jahmeeyah. And the one who says that the Qur'aan, with my recitation is created is from the sect of the Jahmeeyah."*

Sheikh al-Islaam Ibn Taymeeyah said, in his book Minhaaj as-Sunnah, [112]

> *"The way of the people of the Sunnah and adherence to the Jamaa'ah is an old way, established and known among the Muslims before Allaah created Abu Haneefah, and Maalik, and ash-Shaafa'ee, and Ahmad. As it was the way which the Companions took and received from their Prophet, and whoever knowingly opposes that way of theirs is a blameworthy innovator in the view of the people of the Sunnah and adherence to the Jamaa'ah. As they, the people of the Sunnah, stand in agreement that the Consensus of the Companions is considered a definitive proof in the religion, in contrast to validity of the consensus of those just coming after them, which is something disputed.*
>
> *Moreover, Ahmad Ibn Hanbal became well known as a leader in preserving the religion when he was patient and steadfast during the trial of people due to the innovation of falsely claiming the Qur'aan is created. But his becoming well known was not because he came forward individually with a unique statement or brought forth some speech which was new, rather the guidance of the Sunnah, upon which he stood, was something already present and well-known before him and his time. He*

---

[111] as-Sunnah vol. 1 pg 179 with a good chain of narration
[112] Minhaaj as-Sunnah, vol 2, pgs 601-607

however acted according to it and called to it, and was patient with those who put him to trial because of their own separation from it."

It is important to clarify the claim that a specific scholar's individual knowledge or specific way should itself be considered the methodology we must follow or a fundamental proof in Islaam. This misunderstanding is not true even in regard to the scholars of the first three generations. Sheikh Muqbil Ibn Haadee, may Allaah have mercy upon him, explains the proper position towards their statements of knowledge in response to the question directed toward him, **"Are the statements of the Salaf considered a definitive proof in matters?"**

Answer. No, they are not considered a definitive proof. As Allaah, the Most Perfect and the Most High, said, ❦ **Follow what has been sent down unto you from your Lord (the Qur'aan and Prophet Muhammad's Sunnah), and follow not any Auliyaa' (protectors and helpers, etc. who order you to associate partners in worship with Allaah), besides Him (Allaah). Little do you remember!** ❦ *-(Surah al-A'raaf: 3)*

The people, in regard to this matter, stand between positions of blameful negligence and harmful extremism. Among them are one type who rejects their statements completely, saying [They are men and we are men.] Yes, it is true that they were men and we are also just men. Yet, the difference between them and us is like the difference between the heavens and earth. Since we utilize and rely upon their understanding in properly understanding the Book of Allaah and the Sunnah of the Messenger of Allaah, may Allaah's praise and salutation be upon him and his family.

If there was no merit or benefit in utilizing that understanding then the scholars would not have written about it in their works. The scholars would not have mentioned this matter of their understanding, in their writings, such as Ibn Jareer in his commentary of the Qur'aan, and Ibn Abee Shaybah in his compilation al-Musannaf, and similarly 'Abdur-Razzaq in his compilation al-Musannaf, and al-Bayhaqee in his work as-Sunan, as well as other scholars who mentioned the statements of the Salaf themselves in understanding this issue. So someone should neither wrongly say that it doesn't have importance nor that is has no true value. Rather we must benefit from their understanding, it is required and only proper that we understand the Book of Allaah and the Sunnah of the Messenger of Allaah, may Allaah's praise and salutation be upon him and his family, according to their understanding.

But as to whether their individual statements are considered a definitive proof in the religion, then the answer is no, they are not. As Allaah, the Most Perfect and the Most High, **And in whatsoever you differ, the decision thereof is with Allaah (He is the ruling Judge).** *-(Surah ash-Shuraa: 10) and He says,* **And if you differ in anything amongst yourselves, refer it to Allaah and His Messenger, if you believe in Allaah and in the Last Day...** *-(Surah an-Nisaa': 59) and He says* **And verily, this is my Straight Path, so follow it, and follow not other paths,...** *-(Surah al-An'am: 153) and He says* **And whatsoever the Messenger Muhammad gives you, take it, and whatsoever he forbids you, abstain from it ...** *-(Surah al-Hashr:7)*

Whereas another group of people go to a different extreme in this, and absolutely rely upon the statements of individuals from the Salaf, making them a proof in the religion. But this is also a mistake, due to what was just mentioned of evidences indicating that from the Qur'aan. A third type of person are those who say, 'We

> *utilize and turn first to the revealed sources of guidance coming from Allaah, the Most Perfect and the Most High, and then towards the understandings which of our righteous predecessors had of the the Book and the Sunnah."*

Sheikh al-Albaanee, may Allaah have mercy upon him, similarly said,[113]

> *"...another matter is that as for the various transmitted narrations and reports of the Salaf, if they do not compliment and support each other, coming from numerous routes, then it is not proper for someone to take what comes only from one person among them, meaning only from one person from among them among the various different individuals, to take that as a methodology, as they were various different individuals among them. It is not proper for one to take that as a methodology. Then that methodology from one individual perhaps comes to oppose what was well known from the Salaf themselves collectively as a whole..."*

Some examples we might consider to understand the importance of these precise statements of the some of the senior scholars is as follows. If someone were to sit down quietly in front of our beloved Prophet, may the praise and salutations of Allaah be upon him, while he was teaching the people, what Islaam would he teach us? Undoubtedly, he would inform us about the guidance revealed to him. The second is like the example of if we were to sit down with one of the Companions who learned at the hand of the final prophet and were blessed by Allaah to be those who carried Islaam to four corners of the world, what understanding of Islaam would we learn from them? Undoubtedly, they would transmit what the took from the Messenger of transmitted guidance. For this reason, an important question related to what would

---

[113] Silsilaat al-Hudaa wa an-Nur audio tape series no. 666

they teach us, is how would we each individually respond to that transmitted guidance? Would we say, [That is not what my sheikh says!], [That is not what we believe in my country.], [I do not find that among the people of my madhhab!] May Allaah protect us from that. So know, with certainty, that this course is not a course putting forward my personal beliefs or those of any single scholar alone rather as was narrated by Ibn Taymeeyah from one of the earlier scholars,[114]

> *"...This is not simply my own beliefs, nor simply the personal beliefs of someone greater than me. Rather it is that belief which has been taken from Allaah, the Most Glorified and the Most Exalted, and from His Messenger, may Allaah praise and salutations be upon him, and is what the first generations of the Ummah gathered upon and agreed upon.*
>
> *It is taken from the Book of Allaah, and those narrations of Saheeh al-Bukhaaree, Saheeh Muslim, and other books of hadeeth, from those well known reported narrations, and those beliefs which have been affirmed as being held by the first generations of this Ummah."*

This distinguishes our way of respecting and turning to the well known scholars, due to the firm knowledge they possessed, seeking the evidences and proofs, without falling into extremism and partisanship towards them. Sheikh Ahmad Ibn Yahya an-Najmee, may Allaah have mercy upon him, explains the important distinction of always connecting ourselves to the evidences, even when generally standing on evidenced positions from the various people of knowledge. He stated,[115]

> *"When a person stands upon a position of an individual of knowledge position because he observes the correctness and strength of the evidence he has and presents, then he*

[114] Majmua' Fataawaa vol. 3, pg. 203
[115] ad-Durur an-Najmeeyah: pg. 283

is not considered as merely standing with that individual personally, rather he is considered someone who stands with that evidence which he possesses, and this is an acceptable type of blind following."

Each and every striving Muslim, in the face of the storm of raised voices calling him to this or that personal understanding in today's world, or to the alleged requirement to follow "traditional Islaam" regardless of what the Companions followed, should know without any doubt that he must generally learn the original truth of Islaam and its fundamentals, and then be steadfast upon it, not answering and moving towards any unsupported misguided call. The famous scholar Ibn Qutaybah, may Allaah have mercy upon him said, [116]

"May Allaah have mercy upon you, if we were to have a dislike of the people of hadeeth and want to move away from their way and towards desiring the way of people of philosophical rhetoric, wishing some closeness to them, then in truth we are moving away from unity towards disunity and division, away from organized efforts together upon guidance towards separation and isolation, away from good social relations with the believers towards alienation and estrangement, and away from having gathered upon the truth toward differing and disagreement."

This correct way and path is which is taken from the revealed sources, as conveyed and taught to us by the verifying scholars upon the Sunnah, is again similar to if the Prophet were to inform us about something with us directly sitting in front of him, as Indeed Allaah has made clear ❖**Nor does he speak of (his own) desire. It is only a Revelation revealed....**❖-(Surah an-Najm: 3-14). Yet how would we respond? Would we say as many Muslims today say when presented with his guidance in a specific issue,

---
[116] Taaweel Mukhtalif al-Hadeeth pg. 16

[That does not make sense to me], [Or the way I see it...] or [I just feel that...] Would we say that directly to our Prophet when he was informing us of that guidance which Allaah in His mercy sent down for us, if he was directly in front of us? If the answer is no, then the question with the same answer is then why do we do so when being given that which is narrated authentically from him?

One of the primary aims of this book is to help enable those who have consciously chosen Islaam to continue to stand and proceeds upon its guidance, without swerving towards into extremism nor falling into neglectfulness and negligence in either their understanding or practice of Islaam. This is only accomplished in our lives by gaining a sound balanced evidenced understanding initially, then strengthening it gradually and implementing it through the mercy and favor of Allaah. That which we pray Allaah makes a reality for us through learning this religion is that we become truly knowledgable believers, inwardly and outwardly. as Allaah has said,

> *The believers are only those who, when Allaah is mentioned, feel a fear in their hearts and when His Verses are recited to them, they (i.e. the Verses) increase their Faith; and they put their trust in their Lord (Alone); Who perform as-Salaat (the prayers) and spend out of that We have provided for them. It is they who are the believers in truth....* -(Surah al-Anfa'al 2-4)

Imaam Sa'dee explains the meaning of the verse as follows, [117]

> "Those who a characterized by these mentioned characteristics *It is they who are the believers in truth....* because they have joined together between outward Islaam and inward faith, between inward actions and outwards actions, between knowledge and

---
[117] Tayseer page 315

deeds, and between fulfilling the rights of Allaah and fulfilling the rights of Allaah's worshipers."

The Actions of a Worshiper's Heart and Limbs Lead to Success or Failure

It is undoubtedly a sad reality that today many Muslims may feel frustrated with all the difficulties faced by them personally as Muslims and even more so with what the Muslims are facing around the world generally. This causes some to not know exactly where to focus, what issues to make important among their priorities. But as mentioned earlier in an encouraging statement from Sheikh Mohammed Baazmool, the road is clear and it starts with you as the individual, not society as a whole, nor with the ruler, not this or that government.

The study of beneficial works from our past and present scholars, like Usul as-Sunnah, provide us with a firm foundation for truly benefiting ourselves and others, and not blindly turning towards falsely beautified "new solutions" that some individual or groups presents to us. This is even more true due to the trials and afflictions the Muslims are suffering in different parts of the world today. It is essential to remember that the guiding senior scholars offer us sound advice that allows us to put things in their true perspective which benefits us, by enabling us to turn our focus where and towards what we can actually do to please Allaah and benefit the Muslim Ummah, rather than simply blame and complain. Consider this beneficial advice from the esteemed sheikh, the guiding senior scholar Sheikh Saaleh Ibn Fauzaan al-Fauzaan.[118] He was asked, "***Questioner: You are not unaware of what has occurred in Iraq and Syria of the establishment of what they are calling the Islamic state. So what position must we take in light of this effort?***" The esteemed sheikh responded, [119]

---

[118] May Allaah rectify the state of the one today who mentions the senior scholars of our age by name yet chooses to exclude Sheikh Saaleh al-Fauzaan, may Allaah preserve him

[119] From an open sitting recorded on 8-9-1434

"What is obligatory is that you make supplications, that you invoke and beseech Allaah, the Most Perfect and the Most High. As you do not have the ability to do any more than this. So it is upon you to make supplications.

Ask that Allaah, for those Muslims, makes a way out of the tribulation they find themselves within, and that He subdue the disbelievers, the hypocrites, and the enemies of the religion. Yes, this is what you have the ability to do in this situation."

This is a reflection of what the methodology of the Salaf stands upon regarding the way to remove our Ummah from such tribulations that afflict it. Their way calls us to work toward our personal rectification first. Sheikh Ibn as-Sa'dee, may Allaah have mercy upon him, said,[120]

*"From the most beneficial of what may be noted about seeking and realizing good in one's future affairs is using the following supplication which the Prophet used to supplicate with: {**O Allaah, make me upright so that all my affairs are protected, set right for me my worldly matters where my life presently exists, make good for me my Hereafter which is my final home to which I have to return, and facilitate in my life the performing of all types of good, and make death a comfort for me by closing the door to every evil.**}*

*Similar to this is his statement about supplication for those encountering difficulties, {**O Allaah! Your mercy is what I hope for, so do not abandon me to myself for an instant, but put all my affairs in good order for me. There is none worthy of worship except You alone.**}*

If a worshiper of Allaah perseveres in making these supplications which encompass what rectifies his future affairs, both from the aspect of his religion and in his worldly matters, with an attentive focused heart, a

---
[120] al-Wassa'il al-Mufeedah lil Hayyat as-Sa'eedah

> true pure intention, and with those actions which help realize that good, Allaah will make a reality these matters which he supplicated for, hoped for and worked towards, and change his condition to be one of happiness and contentment."

Ibn al-Qayyim, may Allaah have mercy upon him, quotes a narration from ar-Rabee'a Ibn Anas, may Allaah have mercy upon him, that he said,[121]

> "A sign of a worshiper loving Allaah is his frequently remembering and mentioning Him. As no one truly loves something truly except that he frequently mentions it."

This was the way of of the first generations, they proceed upon a path paved with pure intention and sincere acts of worship upon the Sunnah. Sheikh Muhammad Ibn Saaleh al-'Utheimeen, may Allaah have mercy upon him, said,[122]

> "Oh my brother, constantly treat and strive to remedy what is within your heart, such that you are constantly washing and cleaning your heart until it becomes pure."

He, may Allaah have mercy upon him, likewise indicated to the Muslims that this is in fact a commitment to inward rectification, in fact, enabling us to better understand those sins which cause us to lose opportunities for victory and gaining honor in this world,[123]

> "The one who truly has a sound clean heart, then Allaah endows him with the extraordinary insight by which he can recognize those less apparent matters which are transgressions, such that within himself, within his inward feelings, he is not someone pleased and comfortable with entering into them. This is from the blessing of Allaah given to someone."

---

[121] Madaarij as-Saalikeen: vol. 2 pg. 163
[122] From his explanation of Riyaadh as-Saaliheen vol. 1 pg. 52
[123] His explanation of Bulugh al-Maraam: vol. 15 pg. 33

This struggle against our desires not only keeps the individual Muslim from sins, but also leads him towards increasing good. Ibn Taymeeyah, may Allaah have mercy upon him, said, [124]

> *"Everyone whose inward thoughts encourage him to commit a sin, but yet he opposes this and prevents himself from doing that and turns away from it for the sake of Allaah, then Allaah increases him in self-rectification, and in his doing of good, and in his acting with the fear of Allaah due to this."*

Therefore, pushing ourselves as far away as possible from falling into sins and transgressions is joined with the second connected aspect of increasing in actions which are considered obedience to Allaah's guidance, these are the practical realization of our taqwa or fear of Allaah. It also is directly connected to avoiding punishments in this worldly life, like such tribulations in this land or that from the Muslim countries. So all of these things and acts are what will change the condition of the Muslim Ummah. Imaam Ibn al-Qayyim, may Allaah have mercy upon him, said, [125]

> *"The practice of acting in obedience to revealed guidance is a tremendous fortress from Allaah, which the one who enters into it gains two distinct aspects of being protected. He is protected from the punishment of sins that occur in this world, as well as the punishment of sins which occurs in the Hereafter."*

He, may Allaah have mercy upon him, also said,[126]

> *"It is enough to understand the harm and danger of committing sins that among the punishments that reaches the one transgressing is that within his heart the high position of Allaah, the Most High and the Most Sublime, decreases the inward reverence and veneration*

---
[124] Majmu'a al-Fataawa vol.10 page 767
[125] al-Jawaab al-Kaafee page 114
[126] al-Jawaab al-Kaafee pg. 113

towards His greatness and veneration goes down, and the importance and priority towards of giving Allaah his rights fades, all due to his falling into transgressions against Allaah's guidance."

The scholars also remind us of the importance of connecting our inner condition, such as thankfulness, to our outward actions. Ibn Rajab, may Allaah have mercy upon him, said,[127]

"Reflecting one's thankfulness to Allaah upon your limbs means not to make use of any blessing given to you except in a matter which is obedience to Allaah, the Most Glorified and the Most Exalted, and to be warned against using it in something which is a sin and transgression."

Sheikh as-Sa'dee, clarifies for us what is meant by Allaah guiding and directing His worshipers towards good when they have proceeded in the right way with the right manners. In his explanation of the statement of Allaah ﷻ **And He is al-Lateef, the Most Kind and Courteous (to His slaves) All-Aware (of everything).**–(Surah al-Mulk: 14), he says,[128]

The meaning of al-Lateef is that He is the One who acts kindly towards His worshiper, and is his Guardian, such that He directs toward him goodness and excellence from directions he, the worshiper, could never imagine.

Similarly He protects His worshiper from evil and harm, in ways that he, the worshiper, can never truly comprehend and measure. He, Allaah, at times raises one of His worshipers and elevates him to the highest level of excellence, due to reasons beyond that worshiper's recognition and comprehension."

---

[127] Collected Writing of Ibn Rajab: vol.1 pg.350
[128] Tayseer al-Kareem ar-Rahman Fee Tafseer Kalaam al-Manaan, pg 876

An example of this excellence Allaah grants to His close servants who stand firm upon His religion, which is only a result of having a foundation authentic Sharee'ah knowledge and acting upon it, is found in the life of Imaam Ahmad, may Allaah have mercy upon him, Haafidh Abu Nu'aym, may Allaah have mercy upon him, narrated that,[129]

> "We once saw Imaam Ahmad come into the marketplace in Baghdad. He purchased a bundle of wood and then placed it on his shoulder to go. But when the people recognized who he was, the vendors left their activities of buying and selling, the shop owners came out of their different shops, and the people walking in the street stopped where they were and offered him the greetings of salaams.
>
> They said to him, "Let us carry your wood for you." But he waved them away with his hand. His face became red, he lowered his eyes saying, "We are only simple poor people, if Allaah had not decreed that we be placed in front of the people, we would have chosen to be unknown and nameless.""

We should know that Allaah will always support, aid, and strengthen our sincere righteous efforts upon this call to the way of the Companions when we sincerely work and diligently walk in their footsteps, just as the people of the Sunnah in the past centuries did. How excellent is the lesson we find in the life history of Imaam ash-Shaafa'ee in his efforts to raise the Sunnah and turn people away from separation and misguidance towards the uniting guidance of revealed Islaam, [130]

> "Abu al-Fadhl Az-Zajaaj said, When ash-Shaafa'ee settled in Baghdaad there were in the main central masjid more than forty or fifty circles of learning. So

[129] Hilyaat al-Awleeyaah Chapter 9: 181
[130] Tareekh Baghdaad: vol.2, page 68

when he came to Baghdaad he would always go and sit in each circle and say to them, "Allaah said such and such", and "His Messenger said such and such" while the people of these circles would say [Our people say such and such...].

This continued until eventually there remained no gathering of knowledge in the central masjid except for his gathering of knowledge."

This important example serves us as guiding advice about the reward of sincere steadfastness in persevering upon the truth. The distinction of adherence to the fundamentals of the Sunnah is something we can learn from the life of Imaam Ahmad, may Allaah have abundant mercy upon him. Indeed from our Salaf, Talhah al-Baghdaadee said, may Allaah have mercy upon him, said,[131]

"Once I rode with Imaam Ahmad in a ship during a journey. As we proceeded, I found he was someone who was silent for long periods of time. But whenever he spoke, he would say, "Oh Allaah cause us to die upon Islaam and upon the Sunnah."

Lastly, we again find an excellent comprehensive advice from our guiding scholar Sheikh Saaleh al-Fauzaan, may Allaah preserve him and lengthen his life, where he said,[132]

"Remain steadfast upon your religion no matter what that costs you. Do not move away from it due to seeking some worldly benefit, or because of fear of your enemies, since in the end final success is always with those who feared Allaah as commanded."

It is essential to thank and ask Allaah to reward the many scholars and students of knowledge whose beneficial works I quoted and referred to in an effort to make this course more comprehensive. May Allaah increase their

---

[131] Tabaqaat al-Hanabilah: vol. 1 pg 179
[132] Sharh Risaa'il ad-Dalaa'il fee Hukm Mawalaat ahlul-Ashraak: pg. 193

rewards and forgive them and us and enter us all into His Jannah. It should be noted that this is compiled by a student, therefore the shortcomings or errors within should be referred to our noble scholars for clarification, as well as brought to the attention of the publisher as sincere advice so that the evidenced corrections or obligatory amendments that the scholars indicated can be made in future editions and the continuing series.[133]

I clearly and openly request every Muslim or Muslim who is aware of a clear mistake within this course to bring that forth, upon evidences, as certainly this religion is advice and sincerely advising each other. As for one who knowingly conceals a matter of knowledge from a necessary and evidenced correction, for whatever motive that might be, then be assured of the truth of the warning of our Messenger, that the one who is requested but still chooses to conceal knowledge intentionally will wear a brindle of fire on the Day of Judgement. As narrated from the hadeeth of Abu Hurairah, may Allaah be pleased with him, that the Messenger of Allaah, may the praise and salutations of Allaah be upon him, said:

{Whoever is asked about some knowledge that he knows, then he conceals it, he will be bridled with bridle of fire.} [134]

---

[133] Although we often are not able to respond and offer thanks, correspondence with constructive evidenced corrections or beneficial comments from those who have used this course are welcomed, and the senders are thanked for their sincere advice. These can be sent to:
Taalib al-Ilm Educational Resources
P.O. Box 27
Unityville, PA 17774, USA
[134] Jamee`a at-Tirmidhee:2649, Sunan Abu Dawood: 3658, and Sunan Ibn Maajah: 266 and was authenticated by Sheikh al-Albaanee, may Allaah have mercy upon him

The Imaam and verifying scholar Sheikh Ibn Baaz, may Allaah have mercy upon him, explained this serious nature of this transgression saying,[135]

> "...As Allaah, the Most Exalted, says, ❴ **Verily, those who conceal the clear proofs, evidences and the guidance, which We have sent down, after We have made it clear for the people in the Book, they are the ones cursed by Allaah and cursed by the cursers. - Except those who repent and do righteous deeds, and openly declare (the truth which they concealed). Such as these, I will accept their repentance. And I am the One Who accepts repentance, the Most Merciful.** ❵-(Surah al-Baqarah: 159-160)
>
> *It is necessary that the position we take in relation to these two verses be a serious position; as our Lord has warned against the concealing of knowledge, He has threatened the people due to this issue, and cursed that one who engages in that concealment. Then Allaah explains that there is no security from this threat and being cursed for the one who conceals knowledge, except for repentance, rectification, and public clarification.*
>
> *Repentance means to repent from the sin and negligence that one previously committed in concealing knowledge, rectification means that someone personally puts forth every effort within his capacity to correct any situation caused by his concealment, and to publicly clarify that knowledge he possesses or action that he previously concealed for the sake of some immediate worldly benefit or that which was a false explanation. As the one whom Allaah blesses with guidance after being misguided in concealing knowledge, there is no true repentance for him except with such a public clarification, and he cannot be successful except through such an act of repentance.*

---

[135] Majmou' Fataawaa wa Maqallaat vol. 23, page 342

This repentance encompasses several matters: truly regretting what he previously committed of the sin of concealment and refraining from revealing knowledge, truly leaving and abandoning this sin due to the fear of His Lord, the Most Glorified and the Most Exalted, and dreading His punishment. While the third condition is that he resolves not to return to that sin again, in addition to the public clarification of this mistake and rectifying what is possible. As he might take the first step and repent but the people are not aware of this, therefore if he clarifies this publicly to the people he has then fully performed what is necessary and his repentance is complete and correct."

In closing it important to remind my brothers and sisters, that just as our noble scholar Sheikh Muhammad Baazmool, may Allaah preserve him, stated, I say, [136]

"I am deficient, and I openly admit that, in order that no one might wrongly suppose that in terms of what I have written, I comprehend and understand it completely, as having deficiencies and shortcomings are part of my general nature. I ask Allaah for help, assistance, guidance, direction, and success...

...No one should imagine that I fully embody what I have written, in terms of its completeness. As what I write and put forward is what I aspire towards for myself, and what I also desire for others from among my brothers. I hope for that goodness for all of us. This is what I advise them towards, just as I would like the same, from them, directed towards me. I ask Allaah to grant all of us success in being guided to what He loves and is pleased with."

---

[136] From the Facebook page of Sheikh Muhammad Baazmool

Likewise, I say as our dear and noble sheikh the guiding senior scholar Sheikh Ahmad Ibn Yahya an-Najmee, may Allaah have abundant mercy upon him, has stated in his introduction to the book 'al-Fataawa al-Jaleeyah' part 2,

> *"I do not free myself from committing mistakes in this work, as indeed no one is free of this. And I hope from the noble reader that if he encounters something that is obligatory to warn about that they should draw my attention to that as someone whom indeed I would thank, and that they inform me of that mistake, clarifying to me what exactly is the mistake in what was stated and how it conflicts with Sharee'ah evidences. As the brother who advises me will find me as one who submits and yields to the truth, turning towards it.*
>
> *That which I do request from the reader is that they offer supplications for me in my absence.[137] As indeed I am in need of such supplications, that Allaah forgive me sins, and that He give me insight into my shortcomings, and that He bless me with steadfastness upon the truth until I meet him as one clinging even to the very edges of the Sunnah, having proceeded upon the straight methodology and way, and having placed my reliance upon the Most Gracious, the Most Merciful."*

That which is correct from my efforts as a student is from the guidance of Allaah and only through His mercy, and that which is deficient is only from myself and Shaytaan, the accursed enemy of those who believe. May the praise and salutations of Allaah be upon the Messenger of

---

[137] The permissibility of requesting someone living to supplicate for you when done in conformity with the guidelines of the Sharee'ah has been established clearly by the texts of the Qur'aan and Sunnah as explained by the guiding scholars. This is seen in ruling no. 11613 by the Permanent Committee for Scholastic Research & Rulings when they were asked: **What is your view of the one who when someone is leaving him he says to him, "Do not forget me in your supplications." or if that other person is going to Mecca he says to him, "Make supplications for me brother." Is this permissible?**

The answer: It is permissible for a Muslim to request from his brother Muslims that he supplicate for him when traveling to perform 'Umraah or traveling for other reasons. This is only recommending and advising with that which contains good. And the success is from Allaah. May the praise and salutation of Allaah be upon our Prophet, his household, and his Companions.

Allaah, his household, his Companions, and all those who followed his guidance until the Day of Judgement. And all praise is due to Allaah alone, Lord of all the worlds.

Abu Sukhailah Khalil Ibn-Abelahyi
Taalib al-Ilm Educational Resources
the 1st of Ramadhaan, 1439 -
(Corresponding to May 17th, 2018)

(1)

THE CRITERION FOR DISTINGUISHING THE TRUTH AN INDIVIDUAL MUST FOLLOW

Sheikh 'Abdul-'Azeez Ibn 'Abdullah Ibn Baaz, may Allaah have mercy upon him

Question: In our current age, there is a lot of differing between the Muslims, with everyone claiming that he is upon the truth of Islaam. So we need from you, and request graciously, that you provide us with that criterion which enables us to judge and distinguish correctly. By this, meaning that criterion from the Book of Allaah and from the Sunnah of the Messenger of Allaah, may the praise and salutations of Allaah be upon him, which every person can take hold of and advise himself to adhere to and follow.

Answer: The criterion is that you must proceed upon everything guided to by the noble Qur'aan and directed to by the pure Sunnah, that which the Companions and first three generations of the Muslim Ummah proceeded upon, and those guided Muslims who followed upon their path proceeded upon. Turn and look at the statements of the people of knowledge, if you have the understanding and ability to do so, proceed upon the way of the Companions as well as those who followed them in goodness, and judge according to the Sharee'ah of Allaah by adhering to the Book of Allaah and the Sunnah. This is the true way, and this is the path of success. This is what is held as correct, and believed by the people of the Sunnah and adherence to the Jamaa'ah: that we proceed upon whatever the Prophet, may Allaah's praise and salutations be upon him, proceeded upon, and whatever his Companions, may Allaah be pleased with them, proceeded upon; and that we act according to the guidance of the Book of Allaah and the Sunnah of His Messenger, may Allaah's praise and salutations be upon him, being steadfast upon that in our statements, actions, and inward beliefs.

If you do not understand specific matters, then go ask the people of knowledge - the scholars - about them. If someone does not have knowledge of a matter, then he should ask the people of knowledge who are present in his age, asking them. Undertake this by seeking out the people of knowledge and insight, from among the people of the Sunnah and adherence to the Jamaa'ah, those who are known to stand upon what is correct and good. You should ask them about whatever matters you are unsure about or which confuse you.

This is the path to success, that you stand and proceed steadfastly upon the Book of Allaah and the Sunnah of His Messenger, may Allaah's praise and salutations be upon him, in both your statements and deeds. Allaah, the Most Exalted, the Most Magnificent, said in His Tremendous Book, ❴ ***And verily, this is my straight path, so follow it, and follow not (other) paths...*** ❵-(Surah al-An'am: 153) And Allaah the Most High said: ❴ ***Guide us to the Straight Way*** ❵-(Surah Al-Faatihah: 6) And Allaah the Most High said: ❴ ***And if you differ in anything amongst yourselves, refer it to Allaah and His Messenger...*** ❵-(Surah an-Nisaa': 59) Allaah, the Most Exalted, the Most Magnificent, said, ❴ ***And in whatsoever you differ, the decision thereof is with Allaah (He is the ruling Judge)...*** ❵-(Surah ash-Shuraa: 10)

This is Allaah's way and this is the straight path of Islaam, directing all worship to Him alone, having true sincerity of deeds for Him alone, walking upon the same path which the Companions of the Prophet, may Allaah's praise and salutations be upon him, walked upon and were steadfast upon along with their Prophet as well as after his death, the way the people of the Sunnah and adherence to the Jamaa'ah have always followed in statements, deeds, and inward beliefs.

(2)

IMPORTANT ADVICE TOWARDS ADHERING FIRMLY TO THE BOOK OF ALLAAH AND THE PURE SUNNAH

Sheikh Ahmad an-Najmee, may Allaah have mercy upon him[1]

I seek refuge in Allaah from Shaytaan, the accursed. In the name of Allaah, the Most Gracious, the Most Merciful.

All praise is due to Allaah, Lord of all the worlds. May Allaah's praise and salutations be upon the noblest of prophets and messengers our Prophet Muhammad, and upon his family, and all his Companions.

As for what follows:

Indeed Allaah, the Most High, sent to us messengers and revealed books of guidance, and made manifest and clear to His created worshipers on earth the upright path of good, as well as the path of evil and wrongdoing. He placed upon them the obligation of implementing that guidance which their messengers brought to them. Allaah placed upon them the obligation of following their messengers and obeying them in whatever those messengers informed them of from their Lord. The Seal of these messengers from among them was Muhammad, may Allaah's praise and salutations be upon him, whom Allaah made the final messenger, and to whom He sent down the Qur'aan which is the last of the revealed books, being the most prevailing and authoritative book from among them. As such, it is an obligation upon all of the Muslims to become close to and accustom themselves to following the guidance of the Book of the Lord, and accustom themselves to obeying and following their Messenger, may Allaah's praise and salutations be upon him.

---

[1] From a transcribed lecture in the voice of the sheikh

Allaah, the Most High, has clearly commanded those He created for His worship with this, saying ❁ *Follow what has been sent down unto you from your Lord (the Qur'aan and Prophet Muhammad's Sunnah), and follow not any Auliyaa' (protectors and helpers, etc. who order you to associate partners in worship with Allaah), besides Him Allaah. Little do you remember!* (Surah Al-A'raf: 3)

And Allaah, the Most High, said, ❁*Then We have put you (O Muhammad) on a plain way of Our commandment, like the one which We commanded Our Messengers before you. So follow you that (Islaamic Monotheism and its laws), and follow not the desires of those who know not. Verily, they can avail you nothing against Allaah (if He wants to punish you). Verily, the wrongdoers are protectors, helpers to one another, but Allaah is the Walee (Helper, Protector,) of the pious.* (Surah Al-Jaathiyah: 18-19)

And Allaah the Most High said, ❁ *O you who believe! Answer Allaah (by obeying Him) and His Messenger when he calls you to that which will give you life, and know that Allaah comes in between a person and his heart. And verily to Him you shall all be gathered. And fear the affliction which affects not in particular only those of you who do wrong, but it may afflict all the good and the bad people, and know that Allaah is severe in punishment.* (Surah Al-Anfal: 24-25)

And Allaah, the Most High, said, ❁ *And whoever contradicts and opposes the Messenger (Muhammad) after the right path has been shown clearly to him, and follows other than the believers' way, We shall keep him in the path he has chosen, and burn him in Hell - what an evil destination.* (Surah An-Nisaa': 115) .

And Allaah, the Most High, said, ❁ *And verily, this is my Straight Path, so follow it, and follow not other paths, for they will separate you away from His Path..."* (Surah Al-An'am: 153)

As well as similar references from other verses. Therefore, it is obligatory upon every Muslim come to stand upon the Book of Allaah, and upon the Sunnah of Messenger of Allaah, may Allaah's praise and salutations be upon him. Meaning, whatever is authentic from narrations of the Sunnah as determined by the scholars of the sciences of hadeeth -those whose knowledge is taken about transmitters of knowledge, in terms of both criticisms and commendation. Those who do so are those Muslims proceeding upon the straight and correct way.

It is obligatory upon them, meaning it is required that all the worshipers of Allaah, to accustom themselves to following the guidance of the Book of Allaah and the Sunnah of Messenger of Allaah, may Allaah's praise and salutations be upon him. It is also an obligation upon the seekers of knowledge that they read the life history of Messenger of Allaah, may Allaah's praise and salutations be upon him, that they read the various hadeeth narrations found in the two well-known Saheeh collections, as well as what is authentic from the different sunan and musnad hadeeth collections.

And, all praise is due to Allaah, the Sunnah has presently been aided and done a great service by many of the noble scholars, from both the early centuries as well as the later centuries, with the latest of them being Sheikh al-Albaanee, may Allaah have mercy upon him. They have done a tremendous service in the continuous preservation of the Sunnah, in their collective efforts to distinguish the authentic from weak narrations. Similarly, this is also something true of those hadeeth verifiers of specific works who are students at various universities. They have also put forth efforts that serve the Sunnah. As such, it is obligatory for the seekers of knowledge to distinguish, utilizing these others' scholastic efforts, between what is authentic from the Sunnah from that with is not authentic and then act upon and implement whatever is authentic and sound.

It is necessary that they follow and adhere to the people of hadeeth and the leading scholars from the Salaf such as 'Abdullah Ibn Mubaarak, Hamaad Ibn Salamah, Sufyaan ath-Thawree, Sufyaan Ibn Uyaainah, Muhammad Ibn Ishaaq Ibn Khuzaimah, Ibn Jareer, as well as others. It is required that they follow and adhere to the way of the well-known scholars of the science of hadeeth, and the way of the first generations, reading the books that explain the correct beliefs, such as the work Tawheed by Ibn Khuzaimah. Included in this are similar works which gather together different authentic hadeeth narrations connected back to the Prophet, may Allaah's praise and salutations be upon him, as well reading those works which have gathered together the narrations of knowledge from the scholars of the first three generations.

From these later books are such works as al-Ibaanah al-Kubraa by Ibn Batah, Sharh Mashakeel, Sharh Usul Aqeedatul Ahlus-Sunnah wa'al-Jamaa'ah by Imam Laalikaa'ee, and other related books. It is only proper that we direct ourselves towards these books, read them, and explain through them the correct way of the people of following the Sunnah and adherence to the Jamaa'ah, and then following it. This is what is obligatory upon us, oh worshippers of Allaah!

It is not permissible for us to take and follow any statements which oppose or contradict the statement of the Messenger of Allaah, may Allaah's praise and salutations be upon him, or his action, or his Sunnah generally, even if the one who made that statement is from the leading scholars, as there is not anyone who is infallible other than the Messenger of Allaah, may Allaah's praise and salutations be upon him. Infallibility has not been granted to anyone other than the Messenger of Allaah. Indeed, Imaam Maalik, may Allaah have mercy upon him, said, *"Everyone is someone whom we take and accept from his statements and reject and leave some of his statements- except for the one within this grave - indicating the grave of the Messenger of Allaah."* Similarly, Imaam ash-Shaafa'ee, may Allaah have mercy upon him, said, *"If you have my statement and find a hadeeth that opposes it, then take the guidance of the ahadeeth and throw my statement with that which is discarded and tossed away."* Imaam Ahmad, also said, *"Do not simply take from me, nor just take from the statements of Sufyaan, nor so-and-so, or so-and-so, rather generally take from where we have taken from (meaning the source texts."* In this way, we proceed in the way which is correct.

This is the way is sound, such that any individual whose statement agrees with the guidance of the Sunnah, then we accept his statement and adhere to it. In this we stand as those upon sound adherence to the Sunnah. But as for that individual who had opposed the Sunnah, then we reject his statement, and neither adhere to nor follow it. This is something which is obligatory upon every single Muslim, and especially the seekers of Sharee'ah knowledge, it is obligatory upon them that they proceed in this correct and proper way.

This is what I am able to present at this time, and the time of maghrib is close now, with only seven or so minutes left.

May the praise and salutations of Allaah be upon our Prophet Muhammad and upon his family, and his Companions.

(3)

THREE QUESTIONS ON ACQUIRING KNOWLEDGE, RECOGNIZING TRUE SCHOLARS, AND THE MEANING OF METHODOLOGY

Sheikh Zayd Ibn Haadee al-Madkhalee, may Allaah have mercy upon him[1]

The noble sheikh was asked, ***Question 1: As a Muslim, whom should a person take understanding of his religion from?***

Answer: A person should take understanding of his religion from that reliable scholar who is known for steadfastness upon sound beliefs and behavior. Meaning, that scholar who judges according to the Sunnah in all his affairs, in both his statements and taken positions, and who has not been influenced by the different occurrences of innovation in the religion or trials that cause straying away from the truth. Indeed, the first generations of Muslims were the most diligent and attentive in this need to inquire and investigate those they took knowledge from. This is shown clearly within examples of their statements, from more than one of them, that they said: Certain the knowledge is from your religion, so one of you should look and consider whom you take your religion from.

However, related to this discussion, there is detailed guidance which should be pointed out. This is that there are regions of the world and countries in which there is an absence of reliable scholars, but residing there are students of knowledge who are suitable to convey knowledge to others who can be benefited from. As such, it is upon an individual to not be neglectful and miss any opportunity to spend time in the company of one who is a reliable scholar. As we are presently in an age in which it has been made easy to indirectly spend time in the company of the different scholars without having to resort to traveling to distant lands, even if these other ways do not serve as a full substitute to direct study with a scholar. This is done through turning to their lectures, lectures which, in every

[1] From 'Summarized Responses to Ten Questions' transcribed from the voice of the sheikh

single area and branch of Sharee'ah knowledge, encompass the explanations of numerous beneficial books.

Therefore, it is upon the seeker of knowledge to be diligent in spending his time in listening to these beneficial lectures, doing so while taking into consideration the requirement of proceeding by gradual stages in his acquisition of knowledge, and the need to give precedence to the most fundamental matters and subjects before others. As knowledge cannot be grasped all at once, it must be learned step by step going through it necessary stages, stage by stage. Because the one who tries to grab it or pick it up all at once loses it or drops it all at once,' as the well-known saying goes.

The scholars have written works related to the manners and methods of seeking knowledge, clarifying what is the best way to acquire knowledge, describing what subjects should be given precedence and what subjects should by left until a later stage. These works also explain those manners and aspects of excellent character that should be taken on by those engaged in seeking Sharee'ah knowledge, along with various advices which are needed by the one proceeding upon the path of study. As such, we advise those seeking knowledge to give priority to reading from these guiding works before beginning their efforts in undertaking their studies, as in doing so they will be able to enter the matter through its proper door.

Question 2: How can we know who is a reliable scholar?

Answer: An individual can recognize who is a reliable scholar through one of two matters:

Firstly, by their having a reputation for being reliable and having sound knowledge, and this being a matter well-known and spread among the people. As with a reputation among the people that is well-known for sound knowledge, there is no need for an specific recommendation. This was indicated by al-Haafidh al-Iraaqee within his work about the science of hadeeth in a line of poetry that means:

What is correct is that the one well known for soundness

has no need for a specific recommendation consider Maalik Ibn Anas   -star of those who collected narrations of the practice sunnahs.

Secondly, from the paths of knowing who is reliable in terms of his knowledge, is a specific recommendations of the people of knowledge or from some of the people of knowledge, and that they bear witness that he is upon a condition of steadfastness, good standing, and reliability in Sharee'ah knowledge.

Question 3: Is it something obligatory upon us to understand the methodology that we attribute and connect ourselves to or not? Or is it just important that we worship Allaah in our lives as we choose and see fit?

It is an obligation upon every Muslim to understand his religion, and what Allaah has made obligatory upon him in terms of worship, and directing every form of worship to Allaah alone, and what enables steadfastness upon this religion, as well as understanding what he must distance himself from, from those matters that have been prohibited. Along with this is the required understanding of the boundaries that Allaah, how free from any imperfection is He, has put in place for His worshipers, and what He has obligated upon them of correct dealing upon guidance with the creation, from the affairs such as buying, selling, marriage, and contracts.

Additionally, included within it is understanding whom he can take understanding of his religion from, meaning only from those people of knowledge and adherence to the Sunnah, those people of knowledge who proceed upon the correct path, and the clear sound methodology. This is especially true in light of the spread of misguidance, and straying from the truth, which is presently found within the ranks of the Muslim Ummah, and the prevalence of many pretenders who are false claimants to sound Sharee'ah knowledge. All of these subjects are from those matters of the religion, both the small and significant issues among them, which are encompassed within the expression or term "methodology."

Some have restricted the use of this term methodology to refer to some specific issues in the religion, such as for example, the criticism and commendation of individuals, yet this confined use is a restriction which is not proper nor suitable. This fact has been pointed out and indicated by a group of the modern-day people of knowledge.

Yet some of the people of knowledge do use this term, methodology, to designate issues of difference between the various Muslim groups and movements and the people of adherence of the Sunnah. As such, it goes without saying, that this difference about the scope of the term methodology is not one which should lead to blaming or serious agitation between people.

Perhaps what the questioner intended in his question was this last mentioned meaning. Upon this assumption, we say to him that there is no doubt that the differences between the people of the Sunnah and the modern-day groups and movements of misguidance are numerous and an extensive. However gaining knowledge in this area is one which falls under the broader collective obligation which is taken up and handled by those specializing scholars, who have proceeded steadfastly and have extensively established themselves within the fields of knowledge.

So upon this, it is suitable that the seeker of knowledge only take from the knowledge of these differences what is necessary to preserve himself from inadvertently falling into them and becoming entangled in that misguidance those groups have. But as for the matter of putting forth refutations and declarations, then he should not enter into this. As this will preoccupy him from seeking more important knowledge which he has need of, as well as entering him into this before his having reached a level of proficiency and expertise in which he could properly take on and be entrusted with that responsibility. And indeed Allaah is the best of preservers and he is the most merciful of those who are merciful.

Assalaamu aleikum wa rahmatAllaahi wa barakatuhu.

(4)

CONSIDERING THE SCHOLAR OF THE SUNNAH YOUR SHEIKH DUE TO HAVING LISTENED TO HIS LECTURES & HAVING READ HIS BOOKS

BY SHEIKH MUQBIL IBN HAADEE AL-WAADI'EE, MAY ALLAAH HAVE MERCY UPON HIM[1]

Sheikh Muqbil ibn Haadee Al-Waadi'ee, may Allaah have mercy upon him, was asked, *"Do I have the right to say the Sheikh Muqbil Ibn Haadee is my sheikh, since I have listened to some of his lectures or after reading some of his books?"*

He replied: Allaah, the Most Perfect and the Most High, said, ❃ *The believers are nothing else than brothers (in Islamic religion)...*❃-(Surah Al-Hujuraat: 10) So firstly you should say that he is your brother, as Allaah, the Most Perfect and the Most High said, ❃ *...So make reconciliation between your brothers, and fear Allaah, that you may receive mercy.*❃-(Surah Al-Hujuraat: 10) The Prophet, may Allaah's praise and salutation be upon him and his family, said {*A Muslim is the brother of another Muslim he doesn't oppress him, nor does he forsake or abandon him...*} And he said, { *...so be worshipers of Allaah and brothers.*} As such, I am your brother for the sake of Allaah, this is the first matter to make clear.

In regard to the issue whether it is permissible to make this other statement or not, then we mention this first matter beforehand because it was not known previously that they would say for example, from Sheikh 'Alee Ibn Abee Taalib or from Sheikh Abu Bakr, or from Sheikh so-and-so, since certainly ❃ *The believers are nothing else than brothers (in Islamic religion)...*❃-(Surah Al-Hujuraat: 10). In regard to the issue of making this statement itself, then its permissibility is what we have been directed to hold as correct, meaning that doing so is permissible, according to what is apparent. It is acceptable from the direction that from among the known methods of transmission,

[1] From 'Answering the Questioner Regarding the Most Important Issues': pg. 564-565

which has been identified by the scholars in the sciences of hadeeth, is 'wajaadah' or valid indirect transmission of a work of knowledge. By this, meaning that you came across one of my works by means of this specific method. That occurred through your purchasing one of my books in the store, in that general situation where no one denies that the author of that specific work of knowledge, as clearly stated on its cover, is Muqbil Ibn Haadee. Due to this, there is no harm in you making this statement about someone of knowledge, and that in this specific sense he is considered your sheikh, or held to be one of your teachers, as you have benefited from his book indirectly.

Additionally, connected to this specific method of transmission, is the case when an additional permission is also given in relation to indirectly transmitted books. As that permission increases the relative strength of wajaadah, as a method of transmission, since it is by itself considered from the lower levels of how knowledge is authentically transmitted from one person to others. Therefore when that person of knowledge additionally, gives permission for transmitting that book or books, this strengthens the level of this transmission of that work of knowledge. And all praise is due to Allaah, I give my permission to all of you for my works. In fact I further thank you for cooperating upon good, for playing a role in the spreading of books upon the Sunnah, may Allaah reward you all with goodness.

After this, we offer the advice to the questioner, our brother for the sake of Allaah, to give due attention and have diligence in his efforts of seeking knowledge, and not simply remain dependent and reliant upon so-and-so nor upon so-and-so. It is proper that he speaks within himself and determines and aspires to try, if Allaah wills, to become more knowledgeable than Sheikh Muhammad Naasiruddeen al-Albaanee, and more knowledgeable than so-and-so and than so-and-so. And if he isn't able to inwardly encourage himself to reach this high level and strive to become more knowledgeable than him, then he must then encourage himself to be someone who shares this pursuit of knowledge with him, and stands with him in this high endeavor of seeking Sharee'ah knowledge, comes to eventually take from those fundamental sources of Islaam which the people of knowledge take from.

Certainly, right now, what I am doing, within my books, is transmitting the statements of the people of knowledge, from the various books of the people of knowledge. Such that, in regard to my books, if you were to take every transmitted statement and send it back to its original place, then the pages of the books would end up being white and blank. We are from those who transmit from the people of knowledge, and all praise is due to Allaah.

Furthermore, we advise our brother generally, may Allaah reward him with good, to strive to gain true understanding of the religion of Allaah, and to be focused giving true attention to spending time in the sittings of the people of goodness and sound understanding, as well as to having a personal library…

…So be diligent with every diligence, may Allaah bless you with good, in spending time in the sitting of the righteous scholars who work and struggle for the face of Allaah. But if that is not something that is made easy for you then be diligent in acquiring good books, and then continue to strive, so that if Allaah so wills, you will become, by Allaah's permission, more knowledgeable than so-and-so and so-and-so, and all praise is due to Allaah. "

Sheikh Doctor Muhammad Ibn 'Umar Ibn Saalim Baazmool, may Allaah preserve him, mentioned in his series familiarizing us with some of the reliable people of knowledge of our age, [2]

"Sheikh Muqbil ibn Haadee Al-Waadi'ee, may Allaah have mercy upon him,

I only encountered Sheikh Muqbil, may Allaah have mercy upon him, a single time while in the company of Sheikh Rabee'a, may Allaah preserve him. This was when Sheikh Muqbil, may Allaah have mercy upon him, had travelled here for medical treatment and was an honored guest of the Kingdom of Saudi Arabia. He was receiving treatment in the city of Jeddah at the Salam Faqeeh Hospital, I accompanied Sheikh Rabee'a during his visit to him in the hospital. Also, I believe we were accompanied by the teacher Khaalid Baqees and the esteemed Sheikh Fuwaad al-'Umree, if my memory hasn't failed me in this.

I also recall that when Sheikh Rabee'a meet Sheikh Muqbil they each addressed each other by each others full names, and took a moment to look at each other, such that it occurred to me that this may have been the first time they have actually met each other in person, and Allaah knows best.

After this they proceeded to directing some questions to Sheikh Muqbil. What is important is that these were the brief moments in which I encountered and met Sheikh Muqbil, may Allaah have mercy upon him. We left both of them to sit and discuss with each other, Sheikh Muqbil and Sheikh Rabee'a, such that when the visit or occasion had come to an end, they were still sitting next to one another and speaking. We then returned to Mecca by car along with Sheikh Rabee'a.

---

[2] From the series 'With Our Scholars' - No. 20

While we were in the car with the Sheikh, he said about Sheikh Muqbil: '*This man is a mujaahid, one struggling for Allaah's sake. Allaah spread by his hand a significant amount of the guidance of the Sunnah!*'

Related to this I also remember that one of our teachers: Doctor Sayyed al-Hakeem, may Allaah have mercy upon him, was teaching us in the hall or auditorium the subject of hadeeth research, in that year in which the method of the process of preparing for one's master's degree is learned. He had previously been a supervisor of the doctoral thesis of Sheikh Muqbil when he was obtaining his master's degree. So he mentioned to us the details of the scholastic dialog that occurred when Sheikh Muqbil was defending his thesis in front the honorable teacher Doctor Mustapha al-'Adhamee, may Allaah preserve him. He requested that we listen to the recording of that thesis defense and dialog. This was in order to draw our attention to his boldness, courageousness, and clarity upon and for the truth, meaning about Sheikh Muqbil, may Allaah have mercy upon him, along with his uprightness and sincerity in what was apparent in his spoken words. And I do not praise anyone above what Allaah knows about them."

(5)

KNOW WHOM YOU ARE TAKING YOUR RELIGION FROM!

Sheikh Saaleh Ibn Sa'ad as-Suhaymee,
may Allaah preserve him

It is an obligation upon a Muslim not to simply take the understanding of their religion from anyone and everyone, such as everyone, whoever they may be, who appears on one of the various satellite channels intended for Muslims. Even when they claim that they have knowledge and that they stand on the frontlines of the resurgence of Islaam among of the Muslim Ummah. Rather, you must take your knowledge from the guiding cultivating scholars who truthfully realize the guidance of Islaam and correctly implement it.

Take your knowledge from those people of knowledge who protect the Book of Allaah the Most High, by defending and warding away from it: the falsehood of those who exceed the limits of proper understanding, from the incorrect claims of those who nullify the true meaning of its texts, and from the distorted false interpretations of the people who are actually ignorant. Indeed, you must have an understanding of those individuals from whom you should be taking your religion. As Allaah says, ❴ *When there comes to them some matter touching public safety or fear, they make it known among the people, if only they had referred it to the Messenger or to those charged with authority among them, the proper investigators would have understood it from them directly.* ❵-(Surah An-Nisaa': 83) Certainly, knowledge is gained and acquired by studying and learning it. Allaah said ❴ *And it is not proper for the believers to go out to fight Jihaad all together. Of every troop of them, a party only should go forth, that they who are left behind may get instructions in Islamic religion, and that they may warn their people when they return to them, so that they may beware of evil.* ❵-(Surah Al-Tawbah: 122)

For this reason, be warned away from what is found of these entertaining accounts and stories, regardless if they are spread through Internet sites which are full of garbage, or whether they are spread through mucky satellite television channels whose loud barking is heard coming from the country of Qatar. Whether this is found on those satellite channels coming from the East or from the West, regardless of their origin or location, you should rather refer back to the scholars. Oh worshiper of Allaah be cautious of these media sources that are in reality generally sources of garbage and rubbish, be warned against taking from them. Be warned, with a strong warning against taking unsuitable rulings about Matters in Islaam from those worthless individuals wrongly raising their voices as authorities. As this description taken from hadeeth narrations, is appropriate to be applied to many of those who are currently found speaking on these satellite channels.

Therefore, I will mention to you some of the names of the reliable scholars. This is done as a way of providing some valid examples of people of knowledge, without it meaning that it is restricted to just those individuals mentioned. As certainly the scholars and the students of knowledge in this land are, all praise is due to Allaah, many and numerous. So we do not need to turn to these sources where garbage and rubbish is what is often found. At the head of those scholars whom I will mention are:

The members of the Permanent Committee for Scholastic Research & the issuing of Islamic rulings in Saudi Arabia

The esteemed scholar who has the responsibility of issuing general rulings for our entire country, Sheikh 'Abdul-'Azeez Aal-Sheikh, (may Allaah preserve him)

The esteemed Sheikh Saaleh al-Fauzaan, (may Allaah preserve him)

The esteemed Sheikh 'Abdullah Al-Ghudyaan, (may Allaah have mercy upon him)

The notable Sheikh Saaleh ibn Abdul-Azeez Aal-Sheikh, (may Allaah preserve him)

The esteemed Sheikh Rabee'a Ibn Haadee al-Madkhalee, (may Allaah preserve him)

The esteemed Sheikh 'Abdul-Muhsin Ibn Hamd al-'Abbaad, (may Allaah preserve him)

The esteemed Sheikh 'Alee Ibn Naasir Faqeehee, (may Allaah preserve him)

The esteemed Sheikh Ahmad an-Najmee, (may Allaah have mercy upon him)

and our Sheikh Zayd Ibn Haadee, (may Allaah have mercy upon him)

as well as other than these from among the reliable scholars, people of knowledge, and students of knowledge. As I previously stated, these names I have mentioned, are mentioned not for the sake of restricting it to just these individuals, but only so that I can mention to you examples of some of those scholars and students of knowledge who are considered suitable to take your knowledge of Islaam from...

....So know from whom you take understanding of your religion from, a worshiper of Allaah. Be knowledgeable of who today are cultivating scholars. Those who truly base their rulings in Islaam upon the Book of Allaah, the Most High and the Sunnah of His Messenger, may Allaah's praise and salutations be upon him, in the way which conforms to their understanding by the righteous predecessors of the first three generations of believers. Beware of those who are underdeveloped and immature, and beware of those who mistakenly presume to have firm knowledge but in fact lack it. In this subject you can read from the esteemed sheikh, Sheikh Bakr Abu Zayd, the book "The One Presuming to Have Knowledge" and you will benefit from it tremendously. Similarly, read his book, "Jewels for the Seeker of Knowledge" you will benefit from it tremendously, if Allaah so wills.

Also read the book, "The Position of the People of Hadeeth" by our Sheikh Rabee'a, may Allaah preserve him, as well as other beneficial books. Such as the books of Sheikh 'Abdul-Muhsin al-'Abbaad, which, all praise is due to Allaah, are found everywhere in the marketplaces these days. Among his works is an explanation of Imaam an-Nawawee's well known collection of forty hadeeth. Also from his books is the refutation of Farhaan al-Maalikee al-Ismaa'eelee. There are many beneficial works within them, among the most recent of which is a refutation of the terrorists involved in setting off explosions and those misguided individuals who defend them. It is entitled "According to What Intelligence or Understanding of the Religion of Islaam Do you believe that Explosions or Other Acts Of Destruction Could Be Considered Jihaad in the Path of Allaah- Judge Intelligently of Young Muslims" Read this beneficial book by Sheikh 'Abdul-Muhsin al-'Abbaad, and also read the related book by Sheikh Zayd al-Madkhalee entitled "Terrorism." There are also other valuable books the esteemed doctor, Sheikh Sulaymaan

Ibn 'Abdullah Abaa al-Kheel, an administrator at the Imaam Muhammad Ibn Sa'ud Islamic University, which were released recently. These are all beneficial books which explain and clarify the correct methodology of the truth and warn against the many dangerous methodologies of falsehood among the Muslims.

Read from these mentioned books, and you all will benefit from them, if Allaah so wills. While being warned away from the books of those who falsely presume that they have sound comprehension of matters in Islaam, those who wrongly hold that they are proficient and have a good understanding, and those who put forward a great deal of speech but with little actual value. Meaning those who churn out words and produce statements, churning them out in lectures and sermons while it is as if his tongue rolls just as a cow rolls it tongue when chewing. They speak for five or six hours, without any limits or clear direction of what they might discuss. Such people produce little more than buzzing drivel, which, despite its attention drawing noise, just like the horns of two opposing animal's who clash together, you realize is not anything significant and in fact only something which will have little lasting affect.

Sheikh Ahmad a an-Najmee was asked[1]:

"May Allaah grant you good. This questioner from Holland says: Our Sheikh, may Allaah protect you. We have a caller here in Holland who claims that Sheikh 'Ubayd al-Jaabiree, Sheikh Saaleh as-Suhaymee, and Sheikh Muhammad Ibn Haadee are not scholars but in fact are only students of knowledge.

Additionally, when he is brought any statement from Sheikh Rabee'a al-Madkhalee or from one of the other scholars from the people of knowledge, he replies, {I only want the statement of al-'Abbaad (meaning Sheikh 'Abdul-Muhsin al-'Abbaad), as he has more knowledge than these others...}" The presenter starts to begin continue on to an additional question, but is interrupted by Sheikh an-Najmee who says,

"What is apparent is that these statements from this individual, is the speech of someone whose purpose or aim is to remove the scholars of Salafees from being referred to, such that none remain except for one or two. Perhaps, an occasion will come when he eventually says, about the few he left, "I no longer accept them."

What is the specific issue being used to determine your acceptance of them? And who are you to determine this?

The words of this person are the words of someone who is foolish. The one who makes such statements as, ['Ubayd al-Jaabiree, Muhammad Ibn Haadee, and Saaleh as-Suhaymee, are not scholars.] How could someone make this statement?

These men are people of knowledge who have been teaching within the Islamic University for long periods of time, with some of them teaching for twenty years, and others maybe for even longer. Yet disregarding this fact, this one claims that they are not scholars? Who are you, that you could dare make this statement? Are you even

---
[1] From an audio file in the voice of the Sheikh

a person suitable for entering into the area of scholastic criticisms?

In light of this false criticism, this criticism shows that you are in fact one who stubbornly opposes what is correct, that you are foolish, and that you are clearly not from among the people of knowledge.

Yes, these mentioned scholars, are from the scholars of the Sunnah, those whom it is required that you generally adhere to their statements. But in relation to someone possibly making an error, then no one is free from errors, as everyone makes mistakes. Therefore, if a person makes a mistake, it is obligatory that he himself recognize it. Then after this, if someone later indicates his error, he should also acknowledge it and affirm what is the truth."

(6)

THE CORRECT MEANING OF ADHERING TO THE JAMAA'AH

There is no doubt that the beliefs and methodology conveyed to us by Imaam Ahmad Ibn Hanbal, may Allaah have mercy upon him, is that of the Jamaa'ah which the Messenger of Allaaah, may the praise and salutations of Allaah be upon him, commanded us to hold to and not to separate from. One of the most important safeguards, for the Muslim who loves the Sunnah, to protect himself from falling into extremism or slipping into negligence, is adherence to the Jamaa'ah in his specific age and time. The characteristics of the true Jamaa'ah upon the truth has been described and identified to us authentically, not only by the Messenger of Allaah, himself, but also by the scholars past and present. 'Umar Ibn al-Khataab reported that the Messenger of Allaah, may the praise and salutations of Allaah be upon him, generally said,[1]

{The one who wishes to achieve a comfortable life in Jannah, should adhere closely to the Jamaa'ah. As Shaytaan stands close to the single individual, and from two he is further away.}

Yet there is a great deal of confusion today among the Muslims about the correct meaning of this term Jamaa'ah as found in various hadeeth narrations. The Companions and those who walked in their footsteps understood the proper meaning of this term. They held it to be adhering to the original foundation of revealed guidance even if only a few people in your specific place, era, or age of history did so. Sheikh Saaleh Ibn Fauzaan, may Allaah preserve him, was also asked, **"Question, What is intended when we say, the people of the Sunnah and adherence to the Jamaa'ah?"**. He, replied,[2]

"The people of the Sunnah and adherence to the

---

[1] Narrated by Imaam Ahmad in al-Musnad: vol. 1, pg.18 and as-Sunnah of Ibn Abee 'Assim no. 88 with an authentic chain of narration

[2] As found on alfawzan.af.org.sa: No.16583

Jamaa'ah, are those who act upon the Sunnah of the Messenger, may Allaah's praise and salutations be upon him, and stick closely to the body of Muslims united upon the truth. He does not separate himself from them, or break off and distance himself from them in any way. The one who break off or distances himself from the body of Muslims upon the truth, moves towards Hellfire."

It is authentically narrated that Ibn Mas'ood, may Allaah be pleased with him said,[3]

"The Jamaa'ah is what conforms to the truth, even if you are alone."

The guiding scholar Sheikh Saaleh Ibn Fauzaan, may Allaah preserve him, said,[4]

"It is not enough to simply claim that you adhere or hold to the Jamaa'ah of Muslims upon the truth, without there being a reality behind it. The claim by itself is not sufficient."

Imaam as-Sa'dee, may Allaah have mercy upon him, said,[5]

"Towards the end of time there will be an increasing absence of what is good and an infrequent occurrence of those causes for producing good, and there will be an increase in abundance in forms of evil and numerous different causes for bringing about evil. Such that at this stage, those people who adhere firmly to their religion will be the fewest of the few.

These few people, properly following the religion, will certainly find themselves in a situation of difficulty and tremendous hardship, similar to the state of the one

---

[3] Narrated by at-Tirmidhee in his Sunan, vol.4 pg. 46 and al-Laalakaa'ee in his work Sharh Usul Itiqaad Ahlus-Sunnah: vol. 1 pg. 122. Sheikh al-Albaanee declared its chain of narration as authentic in his verification of Mishkaat al-Masaabeeh: vol. 1, pg. 61

[4] Explanation of the Advice and Counsel of the Prophet: pg. 8

[5] Behajat Quloob al-'Abraar

who holds onto a live coal in his hand. This will be due to the strength of those who oppose them, the significant number of misguiding trials, the many misconceptions, doubts, and deviancy that will abound in matters of the religion, the trials of people pursuing desires and becoming absorbed in their pursuit, the turning of many people towards focusing upon worldly pleasures inwardly and outwardly, the general weakness of people's faith in Allaah, and the difficulty of standing alone upon true guidance, due to the very few people who assist and cooperate upon what is good.

However, there are always those who still hold firmly to Allaah's religion, and engage in pushing to the side those impediments and obstacles which none are able to confront and address except the people of insight, knowledge, and certainty in their Islaam, those people of firm emaan or faith, who stand as being from the best of Allaah's creation. They are those who have been elevated many degrees in Allaah's sight, and their capacity for bringing forth good is increased by Him.

As for their general guidance at this difficult time, Allaah guides His Ummah to accustom and reconcile themselves with these demanding circumstances, and to understand that it is something that they must encounter, and that the ones who withstand these difficulties and obstacles, and remain patient in their good practice of the religion and the faith in Allaah, in the face of these different difficulties, then certainly they have with Allaah one of the highest levels and places, and that He will assist them as their Provider and Supporter in every matter that He loves and is pleased with. As certainly His assistance is always at a level matching how much they have devoted themselves to what He loves and has commanded."

Ibn al-Qayyim al-Jawzeeyah, may Allaah have mercy upon him, said in explaining the background and proper meaning of this narration,[6]

"How excellent is a statement which was mentioned Muhammad 'Abdur-Rahman Ibn 'Ismaa'eel who was well known as Abee Shaamah in his work 'al-Hawaadith wal-Bid'ah':

'Concerning that which comes forth of the command to hold firmly to the Jamaa'ah. What is intended by this is holding firmly to the truth and following it, even if those holding onto it are few and those that are opposing the truth are many.'"

Because the truth is that whatever the Jamaa'ah were upon originally in the lifetime of the Prophet, may Allaah the Most High's praise and salutations be upon him, and the period of his Companions. As such we do not look with any true consideration at the numerous individuals who stand upon something originating from the people of falsehood in those times after them.

'Amr Ibn Maymoon al-Awdah, said "I remained the companion of Mu'adh Ibn Jabal while he was in Yemen, may Allaah be pleased with him, and I did not separate from him until eventually we buried him in the earth of the land of Shaam. After my time with him, I became the companion of the one who had the greatest understanding of Islaam after him from among the people, 'Abdullah Ibn Mas'ood, may Allaah be pleased with him.

Once I heard him, meaning Ibn Mas'ood, say, "Hold firmly to the Jamaa'ah as certainly the Hand of Allaah is with the Jamaa'ah." Yet I also heard him say, at another time, "Pray behind those rulers who delay

---

[6] Aid for the Yearning One in Resisting the Attacks of Shaytaan: pg. 74

the ritual salaah from its proper time. Do this by first praying the salaat yourselves in its proper time, as you fulfilling your obligatory duty. Then go and pray with the people collectively behind the rulers, and this will be counted for you as an additional supererogatory prayer."

So I said, "Oh companion of Muhammad, I don't understand what you are telling me." He said "Why is that?" I said, "Previously you commanded me to hold to the Jamaa'ah and cling firmly to it. Yet now, you command me to firstly, at the proper time perform my ritual prayers by myself, fulfilling my obligatory duty. And then afterwards, to also pray with the congregation, headed by those who pushed it back from proper time, as something which will be considered an additional prayer for me?"

He replied, "Oh 'Amr Ibn Maymoon, previously I had believed you to be the most knowledgeable of the people in this area. Do you know what is considered the Jamaa'ah? I replied, "No."

He said, "The majority of people are wrongly considered as the Jamaa'ah, since they may have veered from what is correct. The Jamaa'ah is whatever agrees with the truth, even if you are by yourself and stand alone."

Ibn al-Qayyim al-Jawzeeyah, may Allaah have mercy upon him, also explains the descriptions related and connected to the Jamaa'ah, or the people upon the truth,[7]

"Know that the intended overall meaning of the related Arabic terms: 'consensus upon guidance', 'the proof', 'the mass of gathered Muslims', is certainly those with knowledge who stand upon the truth, even if it is an individual alone, while all of the people of the world

---

[7] I'laam ul Muwaqqi'een 'an Rabb il 'Aalameen vol. 3 page 398

oppose him and that truth....

...Na'eem Ibn Hamaad, said "If that gathered body of Muslims, in your time, turns away from guidance, then it is upon you to remain upon what was followed and held onto before people strayed and turned away from the truth, even if, in doing so, you stand by yourself. As, in that case, you yourself alone become the Jamaa'ah standing upon the truth." This was mentioned by Imaam al-Bayhaqee.

Therefore we see that those opposers to guidance have distorted the correct meaning of Jamaa'ah, by making it indiscriminately mean the majority of Muslims, and considering whatever the majority is upon the proof and criterion of what should be considered correct, labeling that numeric majority as "the Jamaa'ah". In this way, whatever the majority of Muslims are upon is wrongly made the criterion of what is and isn't the Sunnah, and so evidenced guidance of the Sunnah itself comes to be seen as innovation, and what is affirmed as goodness from the transmitted Sunnah is seen as wrong and evil, due to the scarcity of the people who are truly upon that actual Sunnah, and their rarity among people at different times and in different lands.

They wrongly claim, [The one who does something which is considered astray by the majority (of Muslims), Allaah places him in Hellfire due to that straying.] Yet these opposers do not understand that what is in reality considered astray, is whatever opposes the revealed truth. So if all the people stand upon something which opposes the revealed truth, and only one person alone remains upon the original revealed guidance, then they, the majority, are those who have gone astray despite being numerous.

Consider that a majority of people went astray in the time of Ahmad Ibn Hanbal, except for a small number of individuals. As such that small number of people became the Jamaa'ah, in contrast to all of the jurists, the judges, the Khaleefah, and those who followed them upon misguidance, despite their significant number, all of them are considered those who went astray.

Imaam Ahmad alone stood, clarifying the truth of the nature of the Qur'aan, as the Jamaa'ah. Moreover, when the intellects of the various people opposing him could no longer stand up to his position, they then turned and addressed the Khaleefah saying, "Oh Commander of the Faithful, are you and all of your judges, ministers, jurists, and scholars, are all of them upon falsehood, but Ahmad alone, he is the only one considered to be upon the truth?" This was since their corrupt understanding prevented them from considering that this could be an actual possibility.

Then they took him out and whipped and lashed him publicly after he'd been imprisoned for a long period. Indeed, there is none worthy of worship except for Allaah! How similar is the situation today to what happened in the past! This situation is the unavoidable path which will always have to be walked upon by the people upon the Sunnah standing with the Jamaa'ah until they meet their Lord, just as those upon who came before them had to proceed upon it."

(7)

CHOOSE GOOD COMPANIONS OH MEN AND WOMEN OF THE SUNNAH!

Various Scholars

It is always important that whenever in a specific age or place on earth there are only a few people openly adhering to the Sunnah that we carefully consider of the actual beliefs and methodology of any person from the people whom we take as our associates and close companions. Once we personally understand the importance of turning away from those involved or influenced by the methodologies and callers to innovation in Islaam, we must still work to choose our companions carefully as we striving to learn and practice our perfected religion. Shu'ayb ibn Harb, may Allaah have mercy upon him, said,[1]

"Do not sit with other than two types of individual, a person who can teach you something good and beneficial, which you would accept from him, or a man whom you yourself can teach something of goodness to, with him accepting that knowledge from you. Any other kind of individual, turn and leave alone."

Ibn Jamaa'ah, may Allaah the Most High, have mercy upon him, said,[2]

"It is only proper and suitable that the seeker of knowledge does not mix except with those individuals who are beneficial to him or those people who he himself can benefit... ... (He should) not be exposed to the companionship of those who, when they spend time with him, simply enable him to waste his life, and who do not actually benefit him, nor does he benefit them, those who does not help him focus upon that which should be of true concern and priority to him.

For this reason he should go about ending any

---
[1] Safwat as-Sahwaah, pg. 5
[2] Tadhkiraah as-Saame' wal-Mutakalam, pg. 83

companionship with such individuals, who don't benefit him, at the very beginning of their interaction, before their relationship becomes established and something he is used to. Yet what is mandated or required, if such companionship has become established, is that that he turn away from spending time with such people....

...Such that when he chooses a companion, he chooses one who is: a good associate who was righteous, religious, fears Allaah, has piety, is intelligent, someone who brings about significant good, but very little harm, someone who is easy to interact with and argues little, someone who when you forget, he graciously reminds you, and when you bring to mind some matter of good he assists you in realizing it, someone who when you are lacking in determination, comforts, supports, and motivates you, and when you become weary and restless with a decreed trial, encourages you towards needed patience during it."

For this reason the upright scholars of our time advise the striving Muslim to not take as regular associates those who have affiliated themselves to various groups and movements, despite their acceptance of conveying the Sunnah and spreading beneficial knowledge to those whom you know and can benefit. This does not include those who are stubborn opposers to the truth, who are brought the evidences and proofs from the Qur'an, Sunnah, and statements of the Companions, yet reject knowingly.

What we often hear is that [These people are sincere!] in working hard for Islaam upon the methods they have adopted, that [They truly want Islaam and to support the truth!] Indeed, a person is upon the religion and way of his close associate and companions. This is especially important in relation to being able to achieve and gain a good understanding of the knowledge of our religion, as our Salaf taught to us, as we seek companions to help us proceed upon the path of learning and striving to become better Muslims. In this situation, we must chose even more carefully and even more wisely. Sheikh Muhammad Ibn 'Umar Baazmool, discussed this saying,[3]

Someone said the me, "Who should I take as my companion and friend." I responded take as companions the best of people. Those who are from the people of the Sunnah and who stand upon the correct methodology of Islaam.

Do not be deceived only by the excellence of someone's performance of ritual prayer.

Do not be deceived only by someone's fasting Monday's and Thursdays and the recommended White Days of the month.

Do not be deceived only by someone's efforts to stand up and pray at night.

Do not be deceived only by the length of someone's beard or by the shortness of someone's thobe. But carefully weigh and assess his entire state and condition against the criterion of the authentic Sunnah and the correct methodology of Islaam.

*Indeed, don't you recall that it was mentioned describing the outward actions of the misguided sect of the Khawaarij, , {.... **anyone of you would regard his own prayer and fasting as insignificant when compared to their performance of prayers and undertaking fasting.**} But they (the Khawaarij) will pass through and exit from Islaam like an arrow passing through its target, and they will not return to this religion."*

For this reason, if you hear about an individual that

---
[3] From the series 'They Said and I Responded '#23

the people today say about him, [He is a Jaamee.] or [His is a Madkhalee.] then understand that actually he stands upon the correct methodology of Islaam, and take him as a companion.

If you hear about an individual that the people say about him, [He sits with the scholars who only serve the corrupt rulers, and those so called "scholars" of Medinah] then know that the person they refer to generally adheres to and follows the Sunnah, and the way of the Salaf, so take him as companion. Always be aware, that certainly *{A person is upon the religion of his close companions, so look to who you take as your close companion.}*

Sheikh Sulaymaan ar-Ruhaylee, discusses the various types of harmful companions we often unwittingly spend time with. His explanation gives us details about their levels and degrees or harm, as he explained, [4]

"The type of person an individual can sit and spend time with in this world are of different types. There is a type which is blessed, they guide and direct towards what is good and they advise those with them towards that which brings benefits in the affairs of this world and the hereafter. The one who sits with him, it is inevitable that when he leaves the sitting with this type of companion he has certainly received some benefit, as it is not possible to sit with them without getting some degree of benefit.

*This is the righteous sitting companion whom is was said about by the Prophet may the praise and salutations of Allaah be upon him, {**The example of the good sitting companion is like the one who is carrying musk will either give you some perfume as a present, or you will buy some from him, or you will get a good smell from him.**} In the narration either this person grants some*

---

[4] From an audio selection in the voice of the Sheikh

musk as a gift, if he does you received good from him. If he gives you some then the people smell musk from you, and hold you to be someone of a pleasant smell. If he sells you some then he brought good to you, the people then smell this musk from you. Or you simply benefit from gaining a pleasant smell due to you being in his company.

Secondly, then there is a type of person which speaks about worldly matters and affairs, such that you leave their company without having actually benefited, but he is someone who keeps away from falling into talking in a way or about that which was forbidden. With this type of person, an individual leaves his company without anything against him nor anything for him, with Allaah. You do not have anything against you from sitting with him, but neither did you gain anything in your favor from it. But since spending time with this one takes away and wastes one's time, it was the practice of the first generations of Muslims to only infrequently keep this type of company.

They would only sit with them very little except when there was a Sharee'ah benefit to be gained from a specific sitting, such that the sitting would them fall into what was considered the remembrance of Allaah. Meaning that if a person assesses that they is some true benefit in that sitting, like when a worshiper joins a sitting of the people of knowledge, or someone similar to this, then that sitting becomes and falls under the category of the remembrance of Allaah.

Then there is a type a person who speaks about the affairs of the world, and goes on extensively in discussing things, such that the discussion is not preserved to only include permissible matters. That sitting, with this type of person, inevitably includes what is prohibited from backbiting and similar transgressions. This type of person, you should be warned against sitting or spending time with.

Then there is a type who speaks about that which directly corrupts the heart of one who listens, causing it to become hard, and distancing it from what is good and from what is related to goodness. If, for example one of you here now, were you to sit with him and discuss what is happening in your affairs (of attending these gatherings), he wrongly says [By Allaah you are pitiful, and only burdening yourself. After fajr you go to a lesson at this gathering , then after salatul-asr you again have to go to another two lessons, and after maghreb another lesson! By Allaah, if you were to read day and night with them you won't gain any true benefit from all this.] Also like Shaytaan he says [How many of these conferences have you already attended, from the ten that have been held, but you are still trying to learn, attending one after another!] He causes your heart to turn from and causes it to harden towards that which benefits, and so he pushes a person away from good. And this type of individual you are warned against sitting with, with an even stronger warning than the previous type mentioned before it!

Then there is a type of companionship that all one obtains from their companionship is the inciting a person upon sins from the following of his own base desires and a love of transgressing Allaah's limits. This one you'll warned against sitting with them, with an even stronger warning, then the warning to just mentioned previous type of bad companionship. Meaning that when someone sits with this type of individual, he promotes engaging sins and he makes appealing and attractive deeds that are transgressions in Islaam. Likewise, for this type of individual you are warned against sitting with him with an even stronger warning than the types just mentioned previously.

Then there is a type which sitting with him only encourages and fosters among the one who sits with him doubts and misconceptions in the religion, and falling into the area of innovations into Islaam and coming close to the people upon that, and distancing oneself from the people who adhere to the Sunnah. This last one you are warned from sitting with, and any companionship with, with an even stronger warning than that given for all the type which proceeded it. From this type you should flee with the strongest running away and fleeing, rather you should run away from him with more intensity than you would run from a roaming lion. As in sitting with such individuals, there is tremendous serious harm and danger.

As for these types which we have warned against, they are all types of the evil companion. Anyone who sits with these types as companions is sitting with an evil companion. Meaning those evil companions whom the Messenger of Allaah said their example, the evil companion, is the blacksmith. As when sitting with the blacksmith either the sparks and embers from his work will burn holes in your clothes, or you will have from him the unpleasant smell from his work. Meaning that when in his company, inevitably you will always be affected by something negative which will harm you in some way, to some degree, so be warned from him.

The most significant in danger of all these types of evil companion mentioned is the final one mentioned. Here we are speaking here about that one who connects himself to Islaam, the one who leads to you having an attraction to newly invented matters and innovations in

Islaam. He might say, [Just listen to the lecture, listen to it. Those people claim that he is a caller to innovation, but just listen to the lecture, listen and judge it yourself. You are a person with some intelligence, so just listen to his words, listen to the good he has, listen to what he has accomplished.] He brings you closer, and closer to the people of innovation who the people of knowledge have warned against , warned from upon understanding and clarity, using clear evidences and proofs.

He says, [Just listen to the lecture, who turned you away from this -you're someone of intelligence. Listen yourself as you have intelligence, you have a mind so listen to it. Don't simply submit yourself to the view of those scholars who are saying don't listen to them, don't listen to them, don't listen to them!] He is someone who strives brings you closer to the people of innovation, and causes you to become attached to them. He says, [Look, look, at what they have mashAllaah tabarakAllaah...] while always saying it with a nice smile, face, and pleasant demeanor. He turns you away from the reliable scholars from the people of the Sunnah and brings you closer to the people innovate matters into Islaam.

This type is individual is more dangerous to you than your having a terminal disease or cancerous illness, so be warned from this type of associate with the strongest of warning and stay far from them. Indeed, these are from the types of evil companion one might spend time with, where as blessing and goodness is actually to be found in sitting with those types of good people indicated and mentioned by Ibn al-Qayyim, may Allaah, the Most Glorified and the Most Exalted, have mercy upon him."

The guiding scholar Sheikh Saaleh Ibn Fauzaan, may Allaah preserve him, also reminded us that the general case is that,[5]

> *"Sitting with the people of innovation is not something permissible, as they will have a harmful influence upon one."*

And he, may Allaah preserve him, said,[6]

> *"Today we find many of the people abandon and separate themselves from those whom they have a dispute with or differ with in some worldly matters. But as for separating from those who differ with them in the affairs of their very religion, then they consider this of little importance."*

---

[5] The Reality of the Call of Sheikh Muhammad Ibn 'Abdul-Wahaab & Its Influence Within the Muslim World 1-1-1439 9/18/2017

[6] Explanation of the Structured Poem al-Aadab: pg. 191

(8)

SIGNPOSTS FOR THE USE OR ABUSE OF THE INTELLECT IN ISLAAM

Statements gathered from Sheikh Muhammad Ibn 'Umar Baazmool, may Allaah preserve him

It is the sad case often witnessed from many people who consider and have designated themselves, separate from the true scholars, as "Islamic thinkers" or "Islamic writers". In our modern age, they devised a methodology which support both their whims and the misconceptions about Sharee'ah knowledge. Despite how much they read and delve into the sources of knowledge, their false approach and giving of precedence to their intellect and opinions prevents them from properly understanding and excelling as the scholars understand and excel. Sheikh al-Islaam Ibn Taymeeyah, may Allaah have mercy upon him, mentioned that truly understanding revealed guidance, which is the key to successful learning, and is only a result of Allaah facilitating that for those Muslims who turn towards His guidance properly, not in anyway we see fit,[1]

"Indeed, this Ummah has taken on and proceeded to excel in every branch of beneficial knowledge that can be rightly sought after. Yet the benefit from that reaches only the one whom Allaah specifically illuminates that person's heart through what has reached him of knowledge.

While the one whom Allaah prevents from comprehending guidance then simply reading more books achieves nothing for them other than increased confusion and misguidance."

Due to this they often try to falsely attach merit to the misguided way they have stubbornly chosen to proceed upon, in order to have some standing among

---

[1] Majmou' al-Fataawa vol. 10 pg. 665

the Muslims. The following are three statements from Sheikh Muhammad Ibn 'Umar Baazmool, that help us understand and clarify the proper boundaries for the use or abuse of the blessings of our minds and intellects. In the first statement he explains the confusion of this category of people in terms of their misuse of proper role and place of the use of the intellect within the pure Sharee'ah, and how they define and attempt to distinguish themselves as unique, [2]

> *"I directed my attention to and considered the description given to certain individuals that he is a: writer and a thinker. Yet what is it that they intend when using this expression about someone?*
>
> *Do they mean that this individual writes and intellectually thinks, but that others only write without thinking?*
>
> *Do they mean that while this individual is someone who produces writings from the results of his own individual thinking and intellectual efforts, while others are those who merely write and produce statements relying upon transmitted knowledge, and so merely "write" without the aspect of truly deeply thinking? Such that the former, whom they are actually giving preference and higher merit to, is the one characterized with merit as being both a writer and also an intellectual thinker?!*
>
> *Do they mean that this characteristic of being an intellectual thinker is something specific which not everyone can claim, so by him attributing this characteristic to himself, he is distinguished from others who merely write but actually arn't considered among the "intellectual thinkers?*

---

[2] From the Facebook page of Sheikh Muhammad Ibn 'Umar Baazmool 11-21-17

What is strange and questionable about those individuals that, upon examination, one finds about those giving themselves this description, is that he is inevitably from the people who are part of one or another modern innovated Islamic groups or parties claiming to work for Islaam!

Certainly, a person naturally thinks due to the created nature upon which Allaah created him, and his thinking is not simply that intrinsic natural process of thoughts which he is directed to by his created disposition, meaning only related to needs such as eating and drinking, and living with his spouse! Rather his thinking should be built upon those constructive efforts by which a guided individual realizes that his existence within his life, should be lived according to what agrees with what Allaah has decreed (of commands and prohibitions), and so he is someone who adheres to the revealed Sharee'ah!

For this reason I do not hold that we should use this description of intellectual thinker, except for describing that misguided person whose desires have misled him to rely solely on his intellect without relying upon the revealed Sharee'ah of Islaam, and without relying upon that knowledge which is been transmitted from the first generations of believers within this Ummah. As doing so includes the means to wrongly encourage the use of this term among people, specifically from the direction of the one who wishes to praise himself due to choosing this incorrect way."

He, may Allaah preserve him, also discussed one of the fundamental and fatal contradictions of those who rely upon their intellect first and foremost, and try to make this the means to determine the correct principles of Islaam, and so the needed priorities of the Muslims,[3]

> *"One of the inescapable contradictory dilemmas of the person who relies solely upon his intellectual capacity and ability, is that he determines and assesses matters according to his own intellect However, whenever he encounters someone with greater intelligence, his own intellect and its conclusions may be overcome and subjugated by an individual with stronger intellectual capabilities.*
>
> *Likewise that same second person, who intellectually surpassed him, would be similarly defeated when confronted by some third individual who has an even stronger intellectual capacity than them both, meaning the first two individuals. That third individual, overcomes those conclusions which he, the second person, had believed to be correct and superior, since he surpassies the second person's intellectual strength. just as the second person surpassed the first.*
>
> *This situation is inescapable and inevitable, as there is no individual who relies solely upon his personal intellectual capacity who has a perfect infallible intellect, who would then be a final reference for everyone to refer to. This is the meaning of that statement from the first generations of Muslims, "The one who follows intellectual opinions, frequently changes his positions and stances."*
>
> *However, they, meaning the Salaf, did not condemn the role and place of correctly formed intellectual opinions which were put forward in the proper sphere and limited context. It is narrated within the work Jaame'a Bayaan al-'Ilm wa Fadhlihee,[4] "I heard 'Abdaan Ibn 'Uthmaan say, I heard 'Abdullah Ibn al-*

---

[3] From the Facebook page of Sheikh Muhammad Ibn 'Umar Baazmool 10-31-17

[4] vol. 2. pg. 1050, no.2023

Mubaarak, state "Be someone who generally relies upon transmitted narrations of knowledge, and then utilizes directed intellectual opinions for that which further explains to you those guiding hadeeth narrations."

In the same work the following narration states from Shareeh al-Qaadhee, that he said, "The Sunnah preceded and was an authority before these analogies that you make, so adhere to the Sunnah and do not innovate in the religion. As you will not be sent astray as long as you are taking and being guided by the narrations of transmitted knowledge."

In fact, indicating this complimentary role to an even greater degree, it has been mentioned by the verifying scholars that the sound and properly derived intellectual conclusions will agree with that which is authentically transmitted from revealed knowledge. Even more so, it should be said that, there is nothing rightly considered guidance, nor something rightly seen as correct and proper, nor any truly beneficial expressions of intellectually-based conclusions except that they agree and conform to the foundations and guidelines of the revealed Sharee'ah.

It has been mentioned, that the cause of the destruction of the previous nations or Ummah's, was their turning away from the primary guidance of narrations and adherence to reports of revealed knowledge, and instead choosing to rely upon their intellects and follow their unguided intellectual opinions, limited conclusions, and haphazard thoughts. It is also narrated within the work Jaame'a Bayaan al-'Ilm wa Fadhlihee, (vol. 2. pg. 1047, no.2015)

Ibn Wahb said Yahya Ibn Ayyoob informed me, on the authority of Heshaam Ibn 'Urwah, that he heard his father say, "The people of Banee Israa'eel did not stop being upright until there was born among them children from those people's who were conquered and became their captives of war. Those children were the ones who first innovated among them this way of turning to and relying firstly upon intellectual opinions. In this way Banee Israa'eel was misguided and went astray."

Therefore, blindly relying upon the intellect and wrongly giving it precedence over narrations of transmitted revealed knowledge, is a only a vehicle heading straight toward destruction and ruin. Since, the one who gives precedence to his intellect over revelation becomes an enemy and opponent of the authentic practices and of the narrations transmitting that guidance. He cannot truly understand them, nor can his limited intellect grasp the meaning of their guidance, with its imperfect intellectual capacities, so he rejects them as false. He wrongly chooses to follow his intellectual conclusions and his personal opinions, and so ends up misguided, lost, and ruined.

We see commonly that some people falsely believe that every issue or matter must be judged and assessed according to our personal intellectual views and conclusions, and they wrongly claim that the intellect can comprehend and properly assess the value of every matter or issue we face or encounter. Yet the reality of the matter is that, every intellect has deficiencies and shortcomings, no matter whose intellect we are referring to. Certainly, the intellect has a place, position, and role, but it is one which it should not exceed or go beyond those limits. This is just how a human being in his affairs has boundaries and limits that he cannot safely go beyond. The intellect also, in a final sound estimation, is fundamentally based upon restricted observations and the limits of human experience and perceptions."

Moreover Sheikh Muhammad Baazmool, may Allaah preserve him, also offers excellent concrete examples of the misuse of the intellect, by some of those with limited actual knowledge who oppose the methodology and efforts of the people of the Sunnah, to wrongly justify intentionally turning away from specific aspects and positions of guidance found in the Sharee'ah, [5]

From the ways those, who are opponents to the people of the Sunnah, turn away from guidance is by putting forth their false claims or sayings such as:

- *[This is an issue in which there is differences, so chose any of the views you want from the different statements.]*

- *[This ruling is not based upon any verse found in the Qur'aan.]*

- *[The rule in these matters of custom is permissibility.][6]*

- *[The ruling in this issue is only based upon a hadeeth which has a narrator accused of failing to properly name the narrator he took from, as such any statement based upon that hadeeth must not be sound and a proof.]*

- *[This practice is something we should consider permissible due to the benefit gained from it in efforts of calling people to the religion, even if it is indeed prohibited by a revealed source text.]*

- *[The collective objectives of the Sharee'ah are based upon generally respecting this matter, so we do not pay attention to that authentic hadeeth narration*

---

[5] Various Statements 1329 from the sheikh's website
[6] Meaning using this as an excuse, outside the scope of when this principle is applied as explained by the scholars. And Allaah knows best.

which specifically prohibits it.]

- *[Our intellectual determinations do not agree with this hadeeth or with a literal meaning of this verse of the Qur'aan, therefore due to this we must give precedence to our intellectual conclusions before what the source texts apparently indicate.]*

- *[This matter is not something which will be accepted by the general people, and this consideration must be given precedence over other considerations. As if the people are pleased with a matter then consensus is reached, and that consensus is given precedence of the source texts.]*

These are some of the most serious and significant false derivations and distorted conclusions of those who oppose the guidance of the Sunnah. They have fallen into these false conclusions due to a number of reasons.

Among them is that a significant number of those who have these errors are individual who have given their pledge of allegiance to an Islamic political party, who they then must now follow in accepting their specific restricted understanding of the religion, believing only according to what their group understands and accepts, and whatever the leader advocated and puts forward. May Allaah guide us, them, and you, to every matter which He is actually pleased with and loves."

This false way often adopted, by many misguided groups, or movements, is based upon desires and the misuse of the intellect, as opposed the established correct way of assessing what is correct and adhering to it through using our intellects.

THE INTELLECT

(9)

THE POSITION OF ABU BAKR & 'UMAR WITH THE MESSENGER OF ALLAAH

It is something clear from the statements and books of the people of the Sunnah generally that they have always given importance to identifying the reliable scholars and leaders from the Jamaa'ah who remained upon the truth throughout the different periods and centuries of Islamic history.

This is also true for the text of Usul as-Sunnah, but even more so, as Imaam Ahmad identifies and ranks those people who are the roots the Jamaa'ah, meaning the Companions of the Messenger of Allaah, may Allaah be pleased with them all. Along with the general connection of correct Islaam to the understanding and practice of the generation of the Companions, within the text of Usul as-Sunnah, Imam Ahmad, may Alllaah have mercy upon him, purposefully indicated the merit of specific individuals among the Companions by name due to the importance of this in Islaam. By this meaning the importance of recognizing the people of the truth and adherence to the Sunnah in different ages and times, but starting first and foremost with the noble Companions as they are, as stated, the root and foundation of the victorious group of Muslims present until the Day of Judgement.[1]

The acceptance or rejection of affirming these specific statements of merit about the Companions of the Messenger of Allaah, is one of the characteristics that distinguishes the person upon the Sunnah from the misguided person who has fallen into the deceptions and misconceptions of the sects and groups of innovation among the Muslims, who often disparage them collectively or individually.[2] It should be known, that the Messenger of Allaah, indicated to us generally who were the best of generations among humanity after he was sent as the last

[1]   Please refer to Lesson 6 within the course book 'An Educational Course Based Upon Beneficial Answers to Questions On Innovated Methodologies' for further discussion of this area from the words of modern scholars.

[2]   A relevant modern example of this is the disparagement and criticism by Sayyed Qutb against 'Uthmaan ibn 'Affaan, may Allaah be pleased with him as well as against other Companions of the last prophet and messenger.

messenger. He was asked, *"Which of the people is best?"* He, may the praise and salutations of Allaah be upon him, replied,[3]

{Myself and those who stand with me now. Then those who are upon those narrations of knowledge transmitted to them, and then those people after them upon that guidance and knowledge transmitted to them.}

Indeed, one of the distinguishing characteristics of the Muslims upon the Sunnah in the first three generations, as explained by the scholars, is that they followed the Companions in being satisfied with the religion which had been transmitted to them as the Jamaa'ah upon the truth. In doing so they laid down the general foundation for every type of good that the Muslim Ummah would proceed upon in the future, for all humanity. This is in comparison to the misguided groups or sects who were not satisfied, and changed and added to the religion.

Ibn Katheer, may Allaah have mercy upon him, said,[4]

"As for the people who adhere to the Sunnah and remained with the Jamaa'ah then they say: 'Any general action or statement which cannot be affirmed as previously something undertaken by the Companions of the Messenger of Allaah, may Allaah be pleased with them all, is something wrongfully innovated into the religion.'

Due to the fact that if it had been previously considered something good, with a valid basis in the religion, they would have proceeded us in undertaking it in order to do good. This was since they did not leave any matter from the matters of achieving good and bringing about goodness except that they proceeded us in

---

[3] Narrated by narrated in al-Musnad of Imaam Ahmad and it was declared at an acceptable level of authenticity by Sheikh al-Albaanee in Silsilaat al-Hadeeth as-Saheehah narration number 1839

[4] Tafseer Ibn Katheer vol. 4, pg.190

striving for and undertaking it."

So consider, who were the pillars and most important members of that first generation, meaning from the Companions? To begin to answer that question, let us go all the way back to the beginning of Islaam while in Mecca. The noble Companion 'Ammar, may Allaah be pleased with him stated,[5]

"I saw Allaah's Messenger and there was none with him, as Muslims, but five slaves, two women and Abu Bakr (meaning those were the only converts to Islaam then)."

So we know that from these early supporters and followers was Abu Bakr as-Siddeeq, and the many merits and distinctions of Abu Bakr, may Allaah be pleased with him, during that crucial period in Mecca when there were only a handful of Muslims upon the earth, are well known. But here, the reader should take note of an important fact that there are those in the current century like Khomaynee, and those upon his corrupt methodology, wish for the sincere Muslims to ignore, meaning that the very entrance into Islaam of 'Umar Ibn al-Khattab, may Allaah be pleased with him, is a result of the specific supplication to Allaah by the Messenger of Allaah. He, may the praise and salutations of Allaah be upon him, asked Allaah to bless and fortify Islaam through the acceptance of Islaam, of one of two individuals whose entrance into Islaam would undoubtedly strengthen the Muslims generally while they were in Mecca. It is authentically narrated on the authority of 'Abdullah Ibn 'Umar, that the Messenger of Allaah, may the praise and salutations of Allaah be upon him, supplicated,[6]

---

[5] Saheeh al-Bukhaaree: 3660
[6] Sunan at-Tirmidhee: 3514, authenticated by Sheikh al-Albaanee, in Saheeh Sunan at-Tirmidhee: 2907, and narrated in al-Mustadrak of al-Haakim: #4484 where he authenticated it and Imaam adh-Dhahabee later agreed with his authentication of the narration.

{Oh Allaah, give strength and honor to Islaam, through the embracing of Islaam by whichever of these two men is more beloved to you, Abu Jahl, or 'Umar Ibn al-Khattab.} And it was said that the one more beloved was 'Umar.

This high central position of these two noble Companions, began upon distinction and continued so throughout the entire life history of the Prophet of Allaah, upon excellence and distinction. This is despite how such a documented fact must enrage those who have the disease of hating the Companions, those believers whom Allaah Himself praised in the Qur'aan. There are many narrations affirming that the Messenger of Allaah indicated to the Muslims that Abu Bakr and 'Umar, should be held generally as sources of guidance for the Muslims in understanding properly implementing the Qur'aan and Sunnah, and he openly acknowledged their efforts of supporting it with their wealth and defending it with their very lives.

During his own lifetime, the Prophet of Allaah, made clear statements indicating that these two men were individuals of guidance, righteous leadership, and exemplary piety for the Muslims to be aware of and benefit from. Additionally, he further indicated to us that both Abu Bakr and 'Umar, specifically were from the most important people for the Muslims to know, be aware of, and take guidance from after his own death, may the praise and salutations of Allaah be upon him. Let us take some time to look at a few of these distinguishing statements, and consider sincerely what is found within the various authentic narrations. It was narrated by Hudhaifah, may Allaah be pleased with him, [7]

{We were sitting with the Prophet and he said: 'I do not know how long I will be with you, so stick to the two after me,' and he signaled towards Abu Bakr and

---
[7] Jamee`a at-Tirmidhi: 3663 and Ibn Maajah: 97

'Umar.}

Likewise, it was also narrated by Hudhaifah, may Allaah be pleased with him, is a related narration that the Messenger of Allaah, may the praise and salutations of Allaah be upon him, said, [8]

{Follow those who succeed me: Abu Bakr and 'Umar.}

It was also narrated by Ibn Mas'ood, may Allaah be pleased with him, that the Messenger of Allaah said,[9]

{Take as examples the two after me from my Companions, Abu Bakr and 'Umar. And act upon the guidance of 'Ammar, and hold fast to the advice of Ibn Mas'ood.}

The merits of these two beloved leading Companions are found in many different places and multiple contexts within the statements of the Last Prophet and Messenger. He, may the praise and salutations of Allaah be upon him, indicated that Abu Bakr and 'Umar, were models for the Muslims in understanding, affirming, and accepting the true beliefs of Islaam that Allaah revealed to explain past events and miracles from the affairs of the unseen world. As Abu Hurairah, may Allaah be pleased with him, narrated,[10]

"Allaah's Messenger said, {Whilst a shepherd was amongst his sheep, a wolf attacked them and took away a sheep. The shepherd chased it and got that sheep freed from the wolf. The wolf turned towards the shepherd and said, 'Who will guard the sheep on the day of wild animals when it will have no shepherd except myself?}

The people, upon hearing this, said in amazement, "Glorified be Allaah!" The Prophet said,

---

[8] Narrated in the al-Musnad of Imaam Ahmad: vol. 5, pg. 382, and Jamee'a at-Tirmidhee: 3662, It was authenticated by Sheikh al-Albaanee, in: as-Silsilah al-Hadeeth as-Sahihah, vol. 3, pg. 233- Narration 1233

[9] Jamee'a at-Tirmidhi: 3805

[10] Transmitted in Saheeh al-Bukharee: 3690

> *{But I believe in it, and so do Abu Bakr and 'Umar.}*
>
> *Although Abu Bakr and 'Umar were not present there (at the time it was said)."*

They were also present during blessed occurrences and miracles that happened in the time of the Companions, may Allaah be pleased with them all. Jaabir Ibn 'Abdullah, may Allaah be pleased with him, narrated that,[11]

> *My father died and was in debt. I suggested that his creditors take the fruits (i.e. dates) of my garden in lieu of the debt of my father, but they refused the offer, as they thought that the amount of dates would not cover the full debt. So, I went to the Prophet and told him about it. He said (to me),* ***{When you pluck the dates and collect them in the Mirbad (i.e. a place where dates are dried), call me (meaning Allaah's Messenger).}***
>
> *After I did so he came there accompanied by Abu Bakr and 'Umar, and he sat on the dates and invoked Allaah to bless them. Then he said when leaving,* ***{Call your creditors and give them their full rights.}*** *So, I distributed the dates and paid all my father's creditors in full and yet thirteen extra wasqs of dates remained, seven of which were 'Ajwa and six were Laun or six of which were Ajwa and seven were Laun.*
>
> *I later met Allaah's Messenger at sunset and informed him about it. On that he smiled and said,* ***{Go to Abu Bakr and 'Umar and tell them about it.}***
>
> *They said, "We perceived that was going to happen, as Allaah's Messenger did what he did."*

The Messenger of Allaah also indicated that Abu Bakr and 'Umar, were models for the Muslims in strongly focusing upon knowledge and beneficial actions in Islaam and not being distracted by the pursuit of worldly wealth.

[11] Saheeh al-Bukharee: 2709

As Jaabir ibn `Abdullah, may Allaah be pleased with him, also narrated [12]

> "While the Messenger of Allaah was delivering a sermon on Friday, a caravan of merchandise came to Medina. Some of the Companions of the Messenger of Allaah rushed towards it till only twelve persons were left with him, including Abu Bakr and 'Umar; and it was at this occasion that this verse was revealed, ❦ **And when they see merchandise or sport, they break away to it.** ❦

These two exemplary men, may Allaah be pleased with both of them, were also models to be followed and teachers of the details of the proper worship of Allaah, as learned from the Messenger directly in the proper way. The Muslims of the first generation considered them signposts for distinguishing what was correct and what was the proper way to worship directly connected to the previously established practice of the Prophet. Ibn 'Umar, may Allaah be pleased with him, authentically narrated that the Messenger of Allaah said, [13]

> *{Indeed Allaah has put the truth upon the tongue and in the heart of 'Umar.}*

Ibn 'Umar continued on to say in the same narration,

> "No affair occurred among the people, that when they said something about it, and 'Umar also said something about it'" or he said - "Ibn Al-Khattab said something about it" - except that when relevant verses of the Qur'aan were revealed, it agreed with what 'Umar had said in that affair."

---

[12] Saheeh Muslim: 1880 and reported by Abu Ya`la in his Musnad: vol.3, pg. 468, no 1979, with the addition naming of Abu Bakr and 'Umar' as among the twelve who stayed which not found in the narration in Saheeh al-Bukhaaree. Authenticated by Sheikh al-Albaanee, in Silsilaat al-Hadeeth as-Saheehah: vol. 7, pg. 215, no. 3147

[13] Narrated authentically in Jaame'a at-Tirmidhee: 4046, Sunan Abu Dawud: 2962, Sunan Ibn Maajah: 113, al-Musnad of Imaam Ahmad, vol. 2, pg.53, and other collections

Ibn Abee Najib narrated from his father who said:[14]

"Ibn 'Umar was asked about fasting the Day of Arafah (when at Arafat in Mecca). He said:

'I performed Hajj with the Prophet, and he did not fast it, and with Abu Bakr, and he did not fast it, and with 'Umar, and he did not fast it, and with 'Uthmaan, and he did not fast it. I do not fast it, nor order it nor forbid it."

Related to understanding, by practical example, of what is the proper way to perform the ritual prayer, which is from the best of deeds and the very backbone of Islaam, Ibn 'Abdullah bin Mughaffal said about his father,[15]

"If 'Abdullah bin Mughaffal heard any one of us recite aloud: 'In the Name of Allaah, the Most Gracious, the Most Merciful', he would say: 'I prayed behind the Messenger of Allaah and behind Abu Bakr and behind 'Umar-may Allaah be pleased with them both- and I did not hear any of them recite: 'In the Name of Allaah, the Most Gracious, the Most Merciful. aloud"

Likewise, it is narrated from 'Abdur-Rahman bin al-Asam about one of those esteemed young Muslims, Anas Ibn Maalik, who learned the essential acts of worship, both from the Messenger of Allaah, that,[16]

'Anas bin Maalik was asked about the takbir in the prayer. He said: "The takbir should be said when bowing, when prostrating, when raising one's head from prostration and when standing up following the first two rak'ahs.'

Hutaim said: 'From whom did you learn this?' He said:

---

[14] Jamee'a` at-Tirmidhee: 751
[15] Sunan an-Nasa'i: 908
[16] Sunan an-Nasaa'ee: 1179

> *'From the Prophet, Abu Bakr and 'Umar, may Allaah be pleased with them.' Then he fell silent and Hutaim said to him: 'And 'Uthmaan?'*
>
> *He said: 'And 'Uthmaan.'"*

Additionally, Hafs Ibn 'Asim said explaining how their example helped determine the correct position of performing some supererogatory prayers when traveling,[17]

> *I accompanied Ibn 'Umar on the road to Mecca and he led us in two rak'ahs at the noon prayer, then he went forward and we too went along with him to a place where he alighted, and he sat and we sat along with him. He cast a glance to the side where he said prayer and he saw people still standing and asked: What are they doing? I said: They are engaged in glorifying Allaah- meaning offering Sunnah prayer.*
>
> *He said: If I had considered this as the correct way of glorification (when travelling), The amount I would have prayed would have been different. Oh my nephew! I accompanied the Messenger of Allaah on a journey, and he made no addition to two rak'ahs, till Allaah called him. I accompanied Abu Bakr and he made no addition to two rak'ahs till Allaah caused him to die. I accompanied 'Umar and he made no addition to two rak'ahs till Allaah caused him to die. I accompanied 'Uthmaan and he made no addition to two rak'ahs, till Allaah caused him to die,. Indeed Allaah has said,* ❖ **There is a model pattern for you in the Messenger of Allaah** ❖*-(Surah al-Ahzaab: 21).*

Another authentic narration, found in one the six well known collections of hadeeth, Sunan Ibn Maajah, shows both their position, and the clear separation of the Companions from innovation and innovating into the

---

[17] Saheeh Muslim: 1467

religion, Sa'd bin Tareeq said, [18]

> *"I said to my father: 'O my father! You prayed behind the Messenger of Allaah and behind Abu Bakr, 'Umar and 'Uthmaan, and behind 'Alee here in Kufah for about five years. Did they recite Qunut in Fajr?'*
>
> *He said: 'O my son! That is an innovation.'"*

Moreover, Abu Bakr, may Allaah be pleased with him, was someone who would be delegated, by the Messenger of Allaah, to help resolve people's disputes. This is a significant responsibility, yet he was always still diligent to direct the Muslims toward even small matters which would benefit them most in front of their Lord in the Hereafter. As Ibn 'Umar narrated,[19]

> *"al-Agharr (who was a man from Muzayna and had been a Companion of the Prophet) was owed some measures of dates by a man from the Banu 'Amr ibn 'Awf who came to him asking many times. He said,*
>
> *"I went to the Prophet, may Allaah bless him and grant him peace, and he sent Abu Bakr as-Siddiq with me."*
>
> *He continues to say, "Everyone we met on the way greeted us. Eventually Abu Bakr said, 'Don't you know that when people offer the greeting before us, they have gained the greater reward? Give the greeting before them and you will have the greater reward.'"*

The Messenger of Allaah, also indicated to the other Muslims, that both Abu Bakr and 'Umar, were central and indispensable to the believers efforts to establish Islaam and calling others to its guidance during his lifetime. This as also narrated by Ibn 'Umar, may Allaah be pleased with

---

[18] Sunan Ibn Maajah: 1241
[19] Al-Adab Al-Mufrad:984 authenticated by Sheikh al-Albaanee in his verification of the work

him, who said,[20]

> *It was said to the Messenger of Allaah: "Why do not you send Abu Bakr and 'Umar for they are better? He said: {**I cannot do without them, for they are to the religion as hearing and sight from the head.**}"*

After the Messenger's death, may the best of praise and salutations be upon him and his household, they remained upon this excellence of being essential to the well being of Islaam in many ways. This included advising the Muslims to remain steadfast and continue to hold firmly the revealed Book their Prophet had been given, immediately after his death. As Anas bin Maalik, narrated that, [21]

> *He heard 'Umar speaking while standing on the pulpit of the Prophet in the morning (following the death of the Prophet), when the people had sworn allegiance to Abu Bakr. He said the tashahhud before Abu Bakr, and said,*

> *"As for what follows, Allaah has chosen for his Apostle what is with Him (Paradise) rather than what is with you the world. This is that Book (Qur'aan) with which Allaah guided your Apostle, so stick to it, for then you will be guided on the right path as Allaah guided His Apostle with it."*

As the rightly guided successors, they became an additional secondary standard, after the Sunnah, in affirming what was correct in relation to the proper implementation of the guidance of Islaam, just as the Prophet himself had advised. We find it related in Saheeh Muslim on the authority of 'Alee the story of the punishment of al-Walid bin 'Uqbah, where he says,[22]

---

[20] Reported by at-Tabaranee in Al Mu`jam al-Awsaat: no. 4999- authenticated by Sheikh al-Albaanee in Silsilaat al-Hadeeth as-Sahihah: vol. 2, pg.457, no. 815

[21] Saheeh al-Bukharee: 7269

[22] Saheeh Muslim: 1281

> *"The Messenger of Allaah punished with forty lashes, Abu Bakr forty lashes and 'Umar eighty. All of them are in accordance with the Sunnah of the Prophet but this one (the eighty lashes) is preferable to me.*

Similarly 'Umar bin al-Khattab, himself, discussed this consistent practical implementation of Islaam and he wish to safeguard the people from turning away from it,[23]

> *"The Messenger of Allaah stoned, Abu Bakr stoned the married adulterer, and I stoned the married adulterer. If I didn't dislike that I add to the Book of Allaah. I would have written it in the mushaf, for I fear that there will come a people and they will not find it in the Book of Allaah, so they will disbelieve in practicing it."*

The Companions, as part of their methodology, considered these two companions, a reference in determining the permissibility of practices in their day to day affairs of implementing the guidance that had been blessed with. It was narrated that Abu Mujalid said,[24]

> *"Abdullah bin Shaddad and Abu Barzah had a dispute about paying in advance. They sent me to 'Abdullah bin Abu Awfa to ask him about it.*
>
> *He said: 'We used to make payments in advance at the time of the Messenger of Allaah and the time of Abu Bakr and 'Umar, for wheat, barley, raisins and dates, to people who did not yet possess those things.' I asked Ibn Abza, and he said something similar."*

We have been commanded by our Prophet to adhere to their way in everything that agrees with Islaam's guidance, as reflected in the mentioned statement of 'Alee. Sheikh 'Abdul-'Azeez Ibn 'Abdullah ar-Raajhee, may

---

[23] Jamee'a at-Tirmidhee: 1431
[24] Sunan Ibn Maajah: 2282

Allaah preserve him, was asked,[25] ***"What was specifically intended by the Prophet, may Allaah's praise and salutations be upon him, in his statement, {..keep to my Sunnah and to the Sunnah of the Khulafa ar-Rashideen (the rightly guided Khaleefahs)....} until the end of the hadeeth narration? Does this only refer to those four well known Khaleefahs from the Companions? Or does it also include every Khaleefahs, who proceeds upon the same way of the Prophet, may Allaah's praise and salutations be upon him, even if they come in ages after the first period of Islaam.***

*Answer: "What is intended is those four well known Khaleefahs, as they're also, as in another hadeeth narration from the Prophet upon him be Allaah's praise and salutations, {**The Khaleefah after me will be for thirty years.**} Therefore this ended with the period of the Khaleefah of 'Alee, may Allaah be pleased with him. As such we refer back to the Sunnah or practice of the Khulafa ar-Raashideen (the rightly guided caliphs) when there is no clearly established Sunnah from the Messenger, may Allaah's praise and salutations be upon him.*

However if we find a statement from only one of the rightly guided caliphs and it opposes what is affirmed from the Sunnah, then in this situation the Sunnah is what is taken and given precedence. But if, regarding a specific issue, there is no clear text which is affirmed from the Prophet, may Allaah's praise and salutations be upon him, but we have been affirmed statement from one of the rightly guided caliphs, then in this case we take an act upon that statement from that single rightly guided Khaleefah."

---

[25] From His explanation of the work Kitaab as-Sunnah by Imaam al-Barbahaaree, Lecture no. 11

When considering the period of Islaam after the death of the Messenger of Allaah, may the praise and salutations of Allaah be upon him, we see that his steadfastness upon the original guidance of the Prophet of Allaah, prevented 'Umar from seeking a charitable good for the Muslims that his predecessors did not seek to achieve. This is even though it was possible for him to do so, simply because he followed them so closely. As narrated Abu Wail, [26]

> "One day I sat along with Shaiba on the chair inside the Ka`ba. He (Shaiba) said, "No doubt, 'Umar sat at this place and said, 'I intended not to leave any yellow (i.e. gold) or white (i.e. silver) (inside the Ka`ba) undistributed.' I said (to 'Umar),
>
> 'But your two companions (i.e. The Prophet and Abu Bakr) did not do so.' '
>
> Umar said, "Yes, and they are the two persons whom I always follow.' "

Furthermore, there is additional evidence of how closely 'Umar adhered not only to the Sunnah of the Prophet but also the practice of the Khaleefah before him, in the narration from Salim Ibn 'Abdullah from his father who said,[27]

> "It was said to 'Umar bin al-Khattab: 'Perhaps you should endorse your successor.'
>
> He said: 'If I appoint a successor, then indeed Abu Bakr appointed a successor. And if I do not appoint a successor, the Messenger of Allaah did not appoint a successor.'"

Lastly, consider the position of these two pillars among the Companions, in relation to the Hereafter, by looking at what Allaah had informed His Prophet

---

[26] Saheeh al-Bukharee: 1594
[27] Jamee'a at-Tirmidhee: 2225

about their ultimate success on the Day of Judgement. The Messenger of Allaah bore witness that Abu Bakr and 'Umar, were from among those righteous Muslims who it was already testified they were from the most successful in the Hereafter due to their strong emaan inwardly, and outwardly, through their accepting and supporting the call and message of the Messenger of Allaah.

As Sa'id ibn Zayd, may Allaah be pleased with him, narrated, [28]

*"I bear witness to the Messenger of Allaah (peace be upon him) that I heard him say: {**Ten persons will go to Paradise: the Prophet (peace be upon him) will go to Paradise, Abu Bakr will go to Paradise, 'Umar will go to Paradise....**}"*

Abu Sa'id Al Khudree, may Allaah be pleased with him, narrated that the Messenger of Allaah said,[29]

{As for those having higher ranks (in paradise), those having a lower rank will look at them as you look at the stars shining in the horizon of the heaven. Abu Bakr and 'Umar are of those with higher ranks-and how excellent that is!}

---

[28] Reported by Imam Ahmad in al-Musnad: vol. 1, pg. 187, Jamee'a at-Tirmidhee: 3748, Sunan Abu Dawud:4651, Sunan Ibn Maajah : 133 -It was authenticated by Sheikh al-Albaanee in his comments on the well-known explanation of Aqeedatul at-Tahawiyyah: pg. 488 - 489

[29] Reported by Imam Ahmad in al-Musnad: vol. 3, pg. 93, Jamee'a at-Tirmidhee: 3658, Sunan Ibn Maajah : 96 and authenticated by Sheikh al-Albaanee in Saheeh al-Jamee'a`: no. 3793

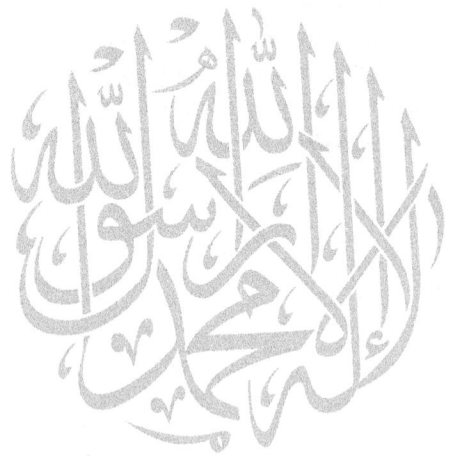

THE NAKHLAH EDUCATIONAL SERIES:

MISSION

The Purpose of the 'Nakhlah Educational Series' is to contribute to the present knowledge based efforts which enable Muslim individuals, families, and communities to understand and learn Islaam and then to develop within and truly live Islaam. Our commitment and goal is to contribute beneficial publications and works that:

Firstly, reflect the priority, message and methodology of all the prophets and messengers sent to humanity, meaning that single revealed message which embodies the very purpose of life, and of human creation. As Allaah the Most High has said,

◈ *We sent a Messenger to every nation ordering them that they should worship Allaah alone, obey Him and make their worship purely for Him, and that they should avoid everything worshipped besides Allaah. So from them there were those whom Allaah guided to His religion, and there were those who were unbelievers for whom misguidance was ordained. So travel through the land and see the destruction that befell those who denied the Messengers and disbelieved.*◈ –(Surah an-Nahl: 36)

TWO ESSENTIAL FOUNDATIONS

Secondly, building upon the above foundation, our commitment is to contributing publications and works which reflect the inherited message and methodology of the acknowledged scholars of the many various branches of Sharee'ah knowledge who stood upon the straight path of preserved guidance in every century and time since the time of our Messenger, may Allaah's praise and salutations be upon him. These people of knowledge, who are the inheritors of the Final Messenger, have always adhered closely to the two revealed sources of guidance: the Book of Allaah and the Sunnah of the Messenger of Allaah- may Allaah's praise and salutations be upon him, upon the united consensus, standing with the body of guided Muslims in every century - preserving and transmitting the true religion generation after generation. Indeed the Messenger of Allaah, may Allaah's praise and salutations be upon him, informed us that, *{ A group of people amongst my Ummah will remain obedient to Allaah's orders. They will not be harmed by those who leave them nor by those who oppose them, until Allaah's command for the Last Day comes upon them while they remain on the right path. }* (Authentically narrated in Saheeh al-Bukhaaree).

The guiding scholar Sheikh Zayd al-Madkhalee, may Allaah protect him, stated in his writing, 'The Well Established Principles of the Way of the First Generations of Muslims: It's Enduring & Excellent Distinct Characteristics' that,

"From among these principles and characteristics is that the methodology of tasfeeyah -or clarification, and tarbeeyah -or education and cultivation- is clearly affirmed and established as a true way coming from the first three generations of Islaam, and is something well known to the people of true merit from among them, as is concluded by considering all the related evidence.

What is intended by tasfeeyah, when referring to it generally, is clarifying that which is the truth from that which is falsehood, what is goodness from that which is harmful and corrupt, and when referring to its specific meanings it is distinguishing the noble Sunnah of the Prophet and the people of the Sunnah from those innovated matters brought into the religion and the people who are supporters of such innovations.

As for what is intended by tarbeeyah, it is calling all of the creation to take on the manners and embrace the excellent character invited to by that guidance revealed to them by their Lord through His worshiper and Messenger Muhammad, may Allaah's praise and salutations be upon him; so that they might have good character, manners, and behavior. As without this they cannot have a good life, nor can they put right their present condition or their final destination. And we seek refuge in Allaah from the evil of not being able to achieve that rectification."

Thus the methodology of the people of standing upon the Prophet's Sunnah, and proceeding upon the 'way of the believers' in every century is reflected in a focus and concern with these two essential matters: tasfeeyah or clarification of what is original, revealed message from the Lord of all the worlds, and tarbeeyah or education and raising of ourselves, our families, and our communities, and our lands upon what has been distinguished to be that true message and path.

Methodology:

The Roles of the Scholars & General Muslims In Raising the New Generation

The priority and focus of the 'Nakhlah Educational Series' is reflected within in the following statements of Sheikh al-Albaanee, may Allaah have mercy upon him:

"As for the other obligation, then I intend by this the education of the young generation upon Islaam purified from all of those impurities we have mentioned, giving them a correct Islamic education from their very earliest years, without any influence of a foreign, disbelieving education."

(Silsilat al-Hadeeth ad-Da'eefah, Introduction page 2.)

"...And since the Messenger of Allaah, may Allaah's praise and salutations be upon him, has indicated that the only cure to remove this state of humiliation that we find ourselves entrenched within, is truly returning back to the religion. Then it is clearly obligatory upon us - through the people of knowledge- to correctly and properly understand the religion in a way that conforms to the sources of the Book of Allaah and the Sunnah, and that we educate and raise a new virtuous, righteous generation upon this."

(Clarification and Cultivation and the Need of the Muslims for Them)

It is essential in discussing our perspective upon this obligation of raising the new generation of Muslims, that we highlight and bring attention to a required pillar of these efforts as indicated by Sheikh al-Albaanee, may Allaah have mercy upon him, and others- in the golden words, *"through the people of knowledge"*. Since something we commonly experience today is that many people have various incorrect understandings of the role that the scholars should have in the life of a Muslim, failing to understand the way in which they fulfill their position as the inheritors of the Messenger of Allaah, may Allaah's praise and salutations be upon him, and stand as those who preserve and enable us to practice the guidance of Islaam.

Similarly the guiding scholar Sheikh 'Abdul-'Azeez Ibn Baaz, may Allaah have mercy upon him, also emphasized this same overall responsibility:

"...It is also upon a Muslim that he struggles diligently in that which will place his worldly affairs in a good state, just as he must also strive in the correcting of his religious affairs and the affairs of his own family. As the people of his household have a significant right over him that he strive diligently in rectifying their affair and guiding them towards goodness, due to the statement of Allaah, the Most Exalted, ❴ ***Oh you who believe! Save yourselves and your families Hellfire whose fuel is men and stones*** ❵ *-(Surah at-Tahreem: 6)*

So it is upon you to strive to correct the affairs of the members of your family. This includes your wife, your children- both male and female- and such as your own brothers. This concerns all of the people in your family, meaning you should strive to teach them the religion, guiding and directing them, and warning them from those matters Allaah has prohibited for us. Because you are the one who is responsible for them as shown in the statement of the Prophet, may Allaah's praise and salutations be upon him, { ***Every one of you is a guardian,*** *and responsible for what is in his custody. The ruler is a guardian of his subjects and responsible for them; a husband is a guardian of his family and is responsible for it; a lady is a guardian of her husband's house and is responsible for it, and a servant is a guardian of his master's property and is responsible for it....}* Then the Messenger of Allaah, may Allaah's praise and salutations be upon him, continued to say, *{...so all of you are guardians and are responsible for those under your authority.}* (Authentically narrated in Saheeh al-Bukhaaree & Muslim)

It is upon us to strive diligently in correcting the affairs of the members of our families, from the aspect of purifying their sincerity of intention for Allaah's sake alone in all of their deeds, and ensuring that they truthfully believe in and follow the Messenger of Allaah, may Allaah's praise and salutations be upon him, their fulfilling the prayer and the other obligations which Allaah the Most Exalted has commanded for us, as well as from the direction of distancing them from everything which Allaah has prohibited.

It is upon every single man and women to give advice to their families about the fulfillment of what is obligatory upon them. Certainly, it is upon the woman as well as upon the man to perform this. In this way our homes become corrected and rectified in regard to the most important and essential matters. Allaah said to His Prophet, may Allaah's praise and salutations be upon him, ❰ **And enjoin the ritual prayers on your family...** ❱ *(Surah Taha: 132) Similarly, Allaah the Most Exalted said to His prophet Ismaa'aeel,* ❰ **And mention in the Book, Ismaa'aeel. Verily, he was true to what he promised, and he was a Messenger, and a Prophet. And he used to enjoin on his family and his people the ritual prayers and the obligatory charity, and his Lord was pleased with him.** ❱ *-(Surah Maryam: 54-55)*

As such, it is only proper that we model ourselves after the prophets and the best of people, and be concerned with the state of the members of our households. Do not be neglectful of them, oh worshipper of Allaah! Regardless of whether it is concerning your wife, your mother, father, grandfather, grandmother, your brothers, or your children; it is upon you to strive diligently in correcting their state and condition..."

(Collection of Various Rulings and Statements- Sheikh 'Abdul-'Azeez Ibn 'Abdullah Ibn Baaz, Vol. 6, page 47)

CONTENT & STRUCTURE:

We hope to contribute works which enable every striving Muslim who acknowledges the proper position of the scholars, to fulfill the recognized duty and obligation which lays upon each one of us to bring the light of Islaam into our own lives as individuals as well as into our homes and among our families. Towards this goal we are committed to developing educational publications and comprehensive educational curriculums -through cooperation with and based upon the works of the scholars of Islaam and the students of knowledge. Works which, with the assistance of Allaah, the Most High, we can utilize to educate and instruct ourselves, our families and our communities upon Islaam in both principle and practice. The publications and works of the Nakhlah Educational Series are divided into the following categories:

Basic: Ages 4- 6
Elementary: Ages 6-11
Secondary: Ages 11-14
High School: Ages 14- Young Adult
General: Young Adult –Adult
Supplementary: All Ages

Publications and works within these stated levels will, with the permission of Allaah, encompass different beneficial areas and subjects, and will be offered in every permissible form of media and medium. As certainly, as the guiding scholar Sheikh Saaleh Fauzaan al-Fauzaan, may Allaah preserve him, has stated,

"Beneficial knowledge is itself divided into two categories. Firstly is that knowledge which is tremendous in its benefit, as it benefits in this world and continues to benefit in the Hereafter. This is religious Sharee'ah knowledge. And secondly, that which is limited and restricted to matters related to the life of this world, such as learning the processes of manufacturing various goods. This is a category of knowledge related specifically to worldly affairs.

…As for the learning of worldly knowledge, such as knowledge of manufacturing, then it is legislated upon us collectively to learn whatever the Muslims have a need for. Yet If they do not have a need for this knowledge, then learning it is a neutral matter upon the condition that it does not compete with or displace any areas of Sharee'ah knowledge…"

("Explanations of the Mistakes of Some Writers'", Pages 10-12)

We ask Allaah, the most High to bless us with success in contributing to the many efforts of our Muslim brothers and sisters committed to raising themselves as individuals and the next generation of our children upon that Islaam which Allaah has perfected and chosen for us, and which He has enabled the guided Muslims to proceed upon in each and every century. We ask him to forgive us, and forgive the Muslim men and the Muslim women, and to guide all the believers to everything He loves and is pleased with. The success is from Allaah, The Most High The Most Exalted, alone and all praise is due to Him.

Abu Sukhailah Khalil Ibn-Abelahyi
Taalib al-Ilm Educational Resources

BOOK PUBLICATION PREVIEW:

30 Days of Guidance:
Learning Fundamental Principles of Islaam [Book 1]

A Short Journey Within the Work al-Ibanah al-Sughrah With
Sheikh 'Abdul-Azeez Ibn 'Abdullah ar-Raajihee
(may Allaah preserve him)

The role of Islaam in today's world is something which is indisputable. Yet there are many different understanding of Islaam from range from dangerous extremism all the way to dangerous laxity which nullifies most beliefs and practices of revealed guidance.

For every Muslim who wishes to live their life in a way pleasing to Allaah it is essential that they ensure that their beliefs and practices actually have evidence and support from within the sources of Islaam. This book approaches this challenge in a way that allows an individual to proceed through discussions related to this- a day at a time over thirty days- based upon the explanation of one of today's steadfast noble scholars.

Compiled and Translated by:
Abu Sukhailah Khalil Ibn-Abelahyi

[Available: **Now** ¦ (SS) $27.50 (DS) $25 (W) $12 ¦ **(Kindle) $9.99**]

BOOK PUBLICATION PREVIEW:

30 Days of Guidance:
Cultivating The Character & Behavior of Islaam [Book 2]

A Short Journey within the Work al-Adab al-Mufrad with
Sheikh Zayd Ibn Haadee al-Madhkhaalee
(may Allaah have mercy on him)

This book is intended for the Muslim individual for self-study, for us as Muslim parents in our essential efforts to educate our children within Islaam and our ongoing endeavor of cultivating them upon the extraordinary character and behavior of our beloved Prophet,
may the praise and salutations of Allaah be upon him.
It is also intended to be an easy to use classroom resource for our Muslim teachers in the every growing numbers of Islamic centers, masjids, and Islamic weekend and full-time schools.

Divided into 30 daily selections of one or more related authentic narrations, it has brief explanations and practical discussions on implementing their guidance in our lives from the well known scholar: Sheikh Zayd Ibn Muhammad Ibn Haadee, may Allaah have mercy upon him.

Compiled and Translated by:
Abu Sukhailah Khalil Ibn-Abelahyi

[Available: **Now** ¦ (SS) $27.50 (DS) $25 (W) $12 ¦
(Kindle) $9.99]

BOOK PUBLICATION PREVIEW:

30 Days of Guidance:
Signposts Towards Rectification & Repentance [Book 3]

A Short Journey Through Selected Questions & Answers With
Sheikh 'Muhammad Ibn Saaleh al-'Utheimeen

(may Allaah have mercy upon him)

*How do I work to save myself from Hellfire? * What should I do, as my society has wrongdoing and many sins? * How can I understand what taqwa is, and how can I have it? * How should I call myself to account as a Muslim?*

*What should be in my heart when I intend to do good? * How can I safeguard my intention for Allaah in everything I do? and more....*

Compiled and Translated by:
Abu Sukhailah Khalil Ibn-Abelahyi

[Available: **Now** ¦ (SS) $27.50 (DS) $25 (W) $12 ¦ (Kindle) $9.99]

BOOK PUBLICATION PREVIEW:

30 Days of Guidance:
Foundations For The New Muslim & Newly Striving Muslim [Book 4]

A Short Journey Selected Questions & Answers With

Sheikh 'Abdul-'Azeez Ibn 'Abdullah Ibn Baaz

(may Allaah have mercy on him)

*What are the conditions of correct Islaam? * What does it mean that Islaam will be strange?* * Is faith only what is in our hearts? * Who is truly considered a Muslim? * When is it necessary for me to ask a scholar? * Is there both free will and Allaah's decree? * What does it mean to worship others as well as Allaah? * Which innovations in Islaam are good? * How can we know who are from the saved sect? * Who is part of that group of victorious Muslims? * Why are there divisions among the Muslims? ...and more*

Compiled and Translated by:
Abu Sukhailah Khalil Ibn-Abelahyi

[Available: **Now** ¦ (SS) $27.50 (DS) $25 (W) $12 ¦
(Kindle) $9.99]

BOOK PUBLICATION PREVIEW:

An Educational Course Based Upon:
Beneficial Answers to Questions On Innovated Methodologies

By the Guiding Scholar
Sheikh Saaleh Ibn Abdullah al-Fauzaan
(may Allaah preserve him)

This course focuses upon the importance of clarity, in the midst of today's confusion, in the way you understand and practice Islaam. But what is the right way or methodology to do so? Examine the evidences and proofs from the sources texts of the Qur'aan and Sunnah and the statements of many scholars explaining them, that connect you directly to the Islaam which the Messenger of Allaah ﷺ taught his Companions, may Allaah be pleased with them all.

Course Features:

Consists of 20 short lessons to facilitate learning and review with several important textual and course appendixes.

Compiled and Translated by:
Abu Sukhailah Khalil Ibn-Abelahyi

[Available: **Now** | pages: 450+ | price: (S) **$30** (H) **$50** | eBook **$9.99**]

BOOK PUBLICATION PREVIEW:
Statements of the Guiding Scholars of Our Age Regarding Books & their Advice to the Beginner Seeker of Knowledge

with Selections from the Following Scholars:

Sheikh 'Abdul-'Azeez ibn 'Abdullah ibn Baaz - Sheikh Muhammad ibn Saaleh al-'Utheimein - Sheikh Muhammad Naasiruddeen al-Albaanee - Sheikh Muqbil ibn Haadee al-Waada'ee - Sheikh 'Abdur-Rahman ibn Naaser as-Sa'adee - Sheikh Muhammad 'Amaan al-Jaamee - Sheikh Muhammad al-Ameen as-Shanqeetee - Sheikh Ahmad ibn Yahya an-Najmee & Sheikh Saaleh al-Fauzaan ibn 'Abdullah al-Fauzaan - Sheikh Saaleh ibn 'Abdul-'Azeez Aal-Sheikh - Sheikh Muhammad ibn 'Abdul-Wahhab al-Wasaabee - Permanent Committee to Scholastic Research & Issuing Of Islamic Rulings

Collected and Translated by Abu Sukhailah Khalil Ibn-Abelahyi al-Amreekee

[Available: **Now** ¦ pages: 370+ ¦ price: (S) **$25** (H) **$37.5** ¦ eBook **$9.99**]

BOOK PUBLICATION PREVIEW:

A Lighthouse of Knowledge From A Guardian of the Sunnah:

Sheikh Rabee'a Ibn Haadee 'Umair al-Madkhalee [Books 1 & 2]

Book 1: Unity, Advice, Brotherhood & the Call to Allaah

Book 2: The Connection with the People of Knowledge, Affairs of Brotherhood & Other Benefits

*Collected and Translated by
Abu Sukhailah Khalil Ibn-Abelahyi al-Amreekee*

[Available: **Now**| pages: **380+** | price: (Soft cover) **$20**
(Hard cover) **$35** eBook **$9.99**]

BOOK PUBLICATION PREVIEW:

Lessons & Benefits From the Two Excellent Works:
**The Belief of Every Muslim &
The Methodology of The Saved Sect**

By the Guiding Scholar
Sheikh Muhammad Ibn Jameel Zaynoo
(may Allaah preserve him)

[Self Study/Teachers Edition]

Course Features:

This course begins with three full lessons with specific practical guidelines on how to effectively study Islaam and gain the knowledge needed to build your life as a Muslim into that which is pleasing to Allaah.

Through twenty lessons on knowledge, beliefs, & methodology along with quizzes, review questions & lesson benefits., the remaining lessons cover several important principles, and the common misconceptions connected to them, which are fundamental to correctly understanding Islaam as it was taught to the Companions of the Messenger of Allaah.

Compiled and Translated by:
Abu Sukhailah Khalil Ibn-Abelahyi

[Available: **Now** ¦ pages: 370+ ¦ price: (S) **$30**
(H) **$45** ¦ eBook **$9.99**]

BOOK PUBLICATION PREVIEW:

Whispers of Paradise (1): A Muslim Woman's Life Journal

[New elegantly designed edition for each year]

An Islamic Daily Journal Which Encourages Reflection & Rectification

12 Monthly calendar pages with beneficial quotations from Ibn Qayyim

Each daily journal page starts with one of the following:

-A Verse from the Noble Qur'aan
-An Authentic Narration of the Messenger of Allaah
-An Authentic Supplication
-A Beneficial Point from a Biography of the Early Generations
-A Beneficial Statement from One of the Well Known Scholars, Past or Present

Daily journal page based upon Islamic calendar (with corresponding C.E. dates)

[Available: **Now** ¦ price: (Soft cover) **$25**]

www.ingramcontent.com/pod-product-compliance
Lightning Source LLC
LaVergne TN
LVHW041250080426
835510LV00009B/667